KB250263

JPLUS

If Korean dramas, movies, K-Pop, cuisine, cosmetics, or fashion piqued your interest in Korea, you might also be intrigued by the idea of traveling to Korea and learning the Korean language. However, the unfamiliar characters and grammar might seem like an intimidating hurdle, making it difficult to take the plunge. Wouldn't it be great if there were just one book that could alleviate that burden?

This book is a travel conversation guide that includes basic greetings, situational expressions, rich local information, and important points to note, enabling even those without any prior knowledge of Korean to enjoy traveling in Korea. It provides Romanized spellings alongside Korean expressions to make it easier to approach the unfamiliar language. It also offers audio recordings of native Korean speakers' pronunciations through QR codes, allowing you to practice conversations well with the audio alone, even without the textbook.

If you utilize the expressions encountered in the book during your actual trip, not only will you have a smoother travel experience, you can also create wonderful, memorable experiences. Hopefully, this book can provide appropriate assistance in situations in which you might need it. Even more, hopefully it can motivate you further in your learning of the Korean language.

　한국 드라마, 영화, K-Pop 또는 한국 음식이나 한국 화장품, 패션 등을 계기로 한국에 관심이 생겼다면 한국 여행과 한국어에도 관심을 갖기 쉽습니다. 하지만 낯선 글자와 문법의 벽이 높아 보여서 시도하기 어려웠을 것입니다. 이럴 때 딱 한 권의 책으로 부담감을 낮출 수 있다면 얼마나 좋을까요?

　이 책은 한국어를 전혀 모르는 사람도 한국 여행을 즐길 수 있도록 기본 인사와 상황별 회화 표현, 그리고 풍부한 현지 정보와 주의할 점 등을 넣은 여행 회화책입니다. 한국어 표현에 로마자 표기법을 함께 제공하여 낯선 언어에 쉽게 다가갈 수 있도록 하였으며, QR 코드를 통해 한국어 네이티브의 발음으로 녹음된 음원을 제공하여 교재 없이 음원만 들어도 충분히 회화 연습을 할 수 있게 하였습니다.

　책에서 접한 표현을 실제로 여행에서 사용할 수 있다면 순조로운 여행이 될 수 있을 뿐만 아니라, 기억에 남을 멋진 추억을 만들 수도 있겠지요. 부디 이 책이 필요한 상황에서 서설한 도움이 될 수 있었으면 좋겠습니다. 더불어 한국어 학습의 동기를 높이는 계기가 될 수 있기를 바랍니다.

07 쇼핑하기 Shopping

08 금융 서비스 Financial services

09 관광하기 Sightseeing

목차 Contents

01

Survival 서바이벌

Essential information to know before departure and
a few key phrases to make your trip enjoyable

1. 여행하기 좋은 한국 Tourist-Friendly Korea

❶ 불이 꺼지지 않는 도시 The City That Never Sleeps

In Korea, many businesses such as convenience stores, cafes, and ATMs operate late into the night or remain open 24 hours a day. Convenience stores, in particular, sell a wide variety of items including basic medicines, stationery, and transportation cards. This means that even if you suddenly need something during your travels, you can easily purchase it.

ⓒ한국관광공사 포토코리아-이범수

❷ 편리한 대중 교통 Convenient Public Transportation

Subways connect various parts of cities, and there are well-established train and bus systems throughout the country. By purchasing a transportation card, you can transfer between buses and subways. Consider planning your trip to Korea using public transportation.

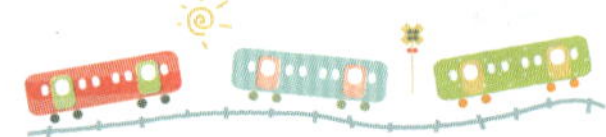

❸ 빠르고 편리한 배달 시스템 Fast and Convenient Delivery System

In Korea, a wide variety of food can be delivered to you quickly and easily. Many famous restaurants also offer delivery services. You can even try having various foods delivered to a park, riverside, or your accommodation. Experiencing Korean delivery service during your trip can be a convenient and enjoyable experience.

Market Kurly   **Coupang**   **Baedal Minjok**

❹ 사계절의 매력 The Charm of Four Seasons

Korea has four distinct seasons, allowing you to enjoy the weather of spring, summer, autumn, and winter. Try some of these activities according to the characteristics of each season. Seasonal festivals are also popular, so don't forget to check local festival schedules at your destination.

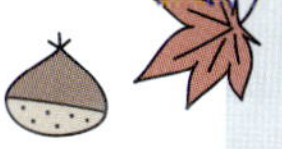

Spring	Cherry blossom viewing (parks, palaces, mountains, camping)
Summer	Water activities (beaches, valleys)
Autumn	Autumn foliage viewing (parks, palaces, mountains, camping)
Winter	Snow sightseeing (ski resorts, sledding hills)

2. 한국은 어떤 나라? Discover Korea

🔵 한국의 지리 Geography of Korea

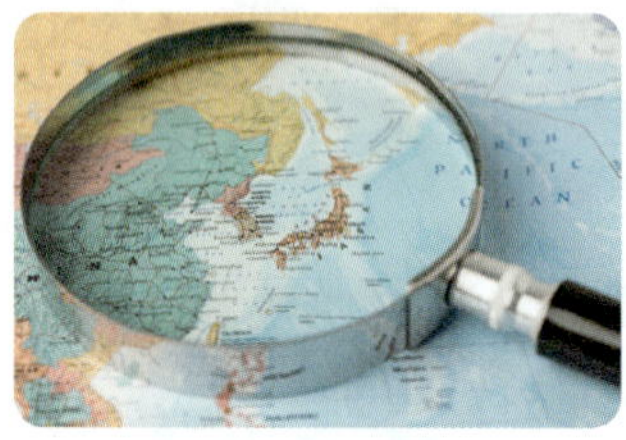

Korea is located in East Asia. The East Sea lies between Korea and Japan, while the West Sea is between Korea and China. The country is called the Korean Peninsula because it is surrounded by water on three sides and shares a land border with China. High mountains are mainly found in the eastern part of Korea, while rivers and plains are more common in the west and south. Among the many mountains, Jirisan Mountain, Seoraksan Mountain, and Hallasan Mountain are particularly famous, with Hallasan Mountain on Jeju Island being the highest mountain in South Korea.

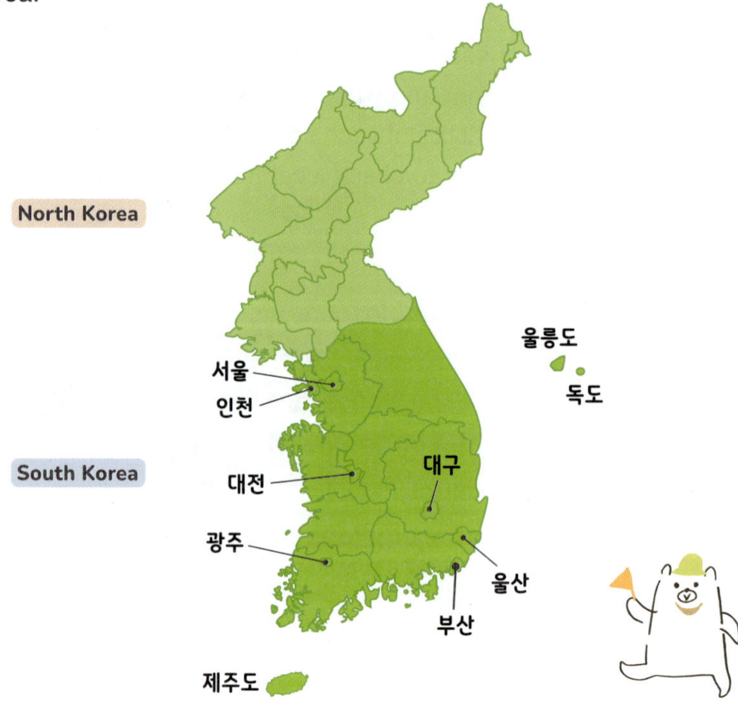

❷ 한국의 공휴일 Korean Public Holidays

Let's look at the Korean public holidays that are relevant when traveling to Korea.

* 신정 New Year's Day (January 1) This day commemorates the first day of the new year. When the new year begins, the bell at Bosingak is rung to announce the start of the new year. Many people go to watch the first sunrise of the new year.

* 구정(설날) Lunar New Year The 1st day of the 1st lunar month is the Lunar New Year. The day before and after are also considered holidays. Families typically gather to eat tteokguk (rice cake soup). Many people travel to their hometowns, so roads are congested and train reservations are difficult to make.

* 어린이날 Children's Day (May 5) On Children's Day, many families with children visit parks, amusement parks, museums, and restaurants. You can enjoy festivals, special events, and special menus for children.

* 추석 Chuseok Chuseok is the 15th day of the 8th lunar month, and the day before and after are also considered holidays. On this day, which was traditionally for sharing harvested food with family, people eat various Chuseok foods such as songpyeon, jeon, and sikhye. Like Lunar New Year, many people travel to their hometowns during this period.

* 크리스마스 Christmas (December 25) Like in many other countries, Christmas trees are decorated and special events are held, making it a good day to enjoy traveling.

3. 한글은 어떻게 읽고 쓸까요?

How do you read and write Korean?

한글이란? What is Hangeul?

Hangeul is Korea's unique writing system, created by King Sejong the Great in the early 15th century during the Joseon Dynasty. Before the invention of Hangeul, Chinese characters were used for writing, making it difficult for  ordinary people with limited education to read or write. Concerned about this situation, King Sejong created Hangeul so that all people could easily read and write.

Because Hangeul letters are based on the shapes of speech organs, they can express many sounds. This gives Hangeul the advantage of being able to phonetically represent most foreign languages, including the English alphabet. As it was designed to allow ordinary people to easily express their thoughts in writing, Hangeul is relatively easy to learn. It consists of 40 characters in total, comprising 19 consonants and 21 vowels.

❶ 모음 Vowels

The vowels in Hangeul were created by combining the symbols '·', '—', and '丨', which represent heaven, earth, and humans, respectively. There are a total of 21 vowels, consisting of 10 single vowels and 11 diphthongs (compound vowels).

ㅏ	ㅓ	ㅗ	ㅜ	ㅡ	ㅣ	ㅐ	ㅔ	ㅚ	ㅟ	Single vowels
[a]	[eo]	[o]	[u]	[eu]	[i]	[ae]	[e]	[oe]	[wi]	
ㅑ	ㅕ	ㅛ	ㅠ			ㅒ	ㅖ			Dipthongs
[ya]	[yeo]	[yo]	[yu]			[yae]	[ye]			
ㅘ	ㅝ			ㅢ		ㅙ	ㅞ			
[wa]	[wo]			[ui]		[wae]	[we]			

Tip "ㅐ and ㅔ", "ㅒ and ㅖ", and "ㅙ and ㅞ" are so similar in pronunciation that Koreans rarely distinguish between them.

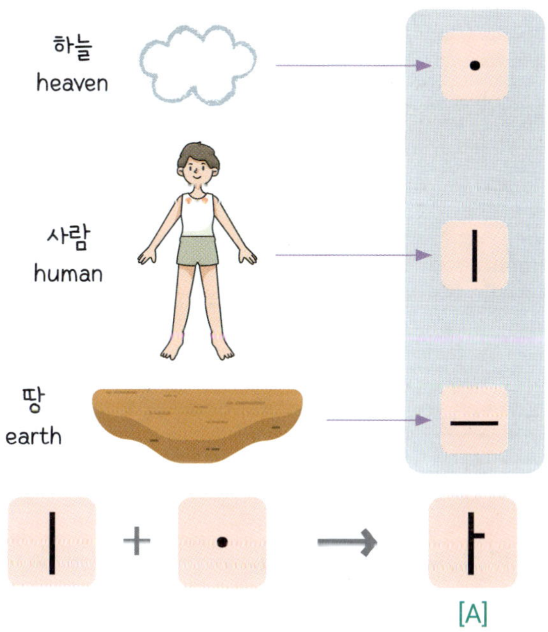

❷ 자음 Consonants

The consonants in Hangeul were created based on the shapes of the vocal organs used to produce sounds. The basic letters ㄱ, ㄴ, ㅁ, ㅅ, ㅇ were used as a foundation, and other consonants were created by adding strokes to these basic shapes. Consonants cannot be pronounced alone and must be used in combination with vowels. There are two types of consonants in Hangeul: basic consonants and double consonants.

Basic consonants	ㄱ	ㄴ	ㅁ	ㅅ	ㅇ
	[k], [g]	[n]	[m]	[s]	[ø] (silent)
Added strokes		ㄷ	ㅂ	ㅈ	
		[t], [d]	[p], [b]	[j]	
	ㅋ	ㅌ	ㅍ	ㅊ	ㅎ
	[k]	[t]	[p]	[ch]	[h]
Double consonants	ㄲ	ㄸ	ㅃ	ㅆ	
	[kk]	[tt]	[pp]	[ss]	
				ㅉ	
				[jj]	
Modified letters	ㄹ				
	[l], [r]				

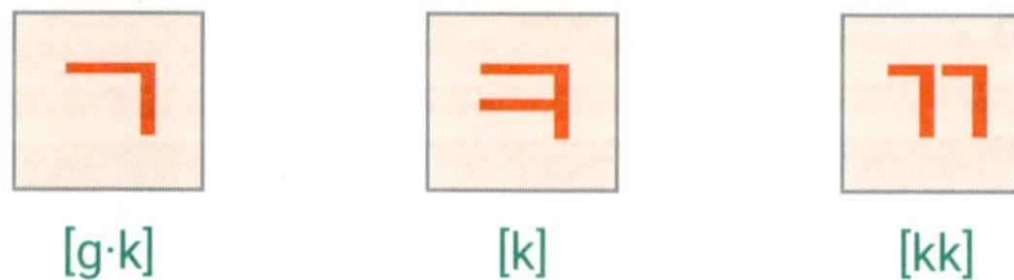

[g·k]　　　　[k]　　　　[kk]

❸ 자음과 모음의 결합 Combination of Consonants and Vowels

In English, when writing the word 한글 ("hangeul") in Roman letters, consonants and vowels are placed side by side. However, in Korean, the word 한글 is constructed by stacking consonants and vowels according to initial and final sounds.

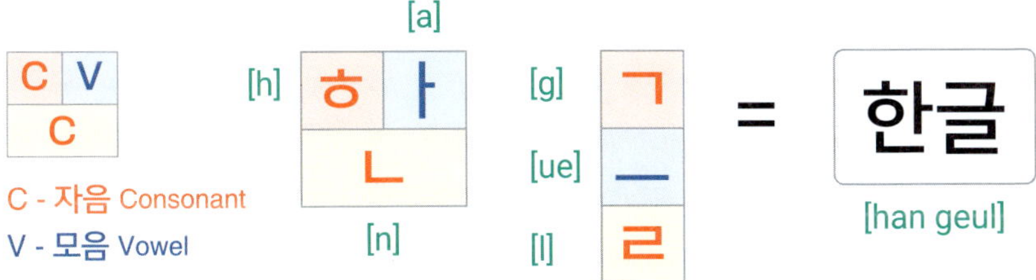

(1) Writing vowels without consonants V

When a syllable starts with a vowel sound and has no initial consonant, the silent consonant ㅇ (called "ieung") is used as a placeholder. This silent consonant is written together with the vowel.

(2) When writing consonants and vowels together C V

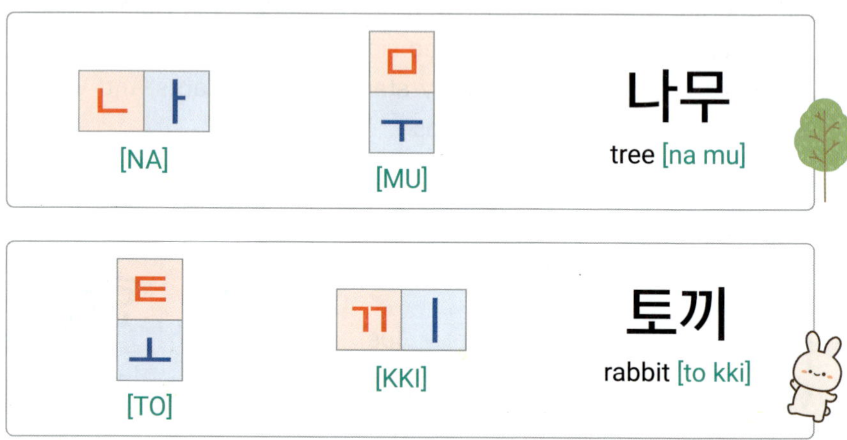

[NA]

[MU]

나무

tree [na mu]

[TO]

[KKI]

토끼

rabbit [to kki]

(3) When there is a final consonant ("batchim") C V C

Batchim refers to the consonant used as the final sound in a syllable. The batchim should be positioned at the bottom of a character that combines a consonant and a vowel. Characters without a batchim, like 아기 [agi], end with a vowel sound, while characters with a batchim, such as 밥 [bap], end with a consonant sound.

Be careful to read these consonants as follows when they are used as final consonants.

ㄱ [k]	ㄱ, ㄲ, ㅋ
ㄴ [n]	ㄴ
ㄷ [t]	ㄷ, ㅌ, ㅅ, ㅆ, ㅈ, ㅊ, ㅎ
ㄹ [l]	ㄹ
ㅁ [m]	ㅁ
ㅂ [p]	ㅂ, ㅍ
ㅇ [ng]	ㅇ

밥

rice [bap]

공

ball [gong]

Exercise:

(4) Double final consonants

Although most final consonants use only one consonant, when two are used, it is called a double final consonant.

ㄲ = ㅋ = ㄱ [k] ㅆ = ㅅ = ㄷ [t]	ㄵ, ㄶ, ㄼ, ㅄ = Pronounce the first letter only 첫 번째 글자만 읽기 ㄹㄱ, ㄹㅁ = Pronounce the second letter only 두 번째 글자만 읽기

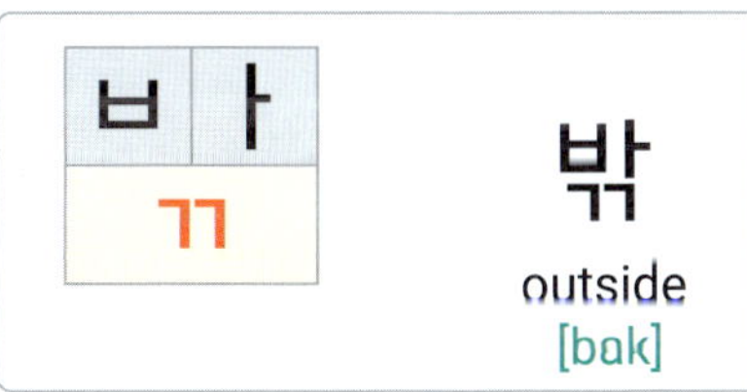

Hello.

안녕하세요.
Annyeonghaseyo.

I'm pleased to meet you.

반갑습니다.
Bangapseumnida.

How do you do?

처음 뵙겠습니다.
Cheo-eum boepgetseumnida.

I hope we get along well.

잘 부탁 드립니다.
Jal butak deurimnida.

Long time no see.

오랜만이에요.
Oraenmanieyo.

How have you been?

잘 지내셨어요?
Jal jinaesyeosseoyo?

I'll see you around.

다음에 또 봐요.
Da-eume tto bwayo.

> **Tip**
>
> The romanization system is written differently from the pronunciation of each Korean letter because it applies various rules of Korean pronunciation.

See you tomorrow.

내일 봐요.
Naeil bwayo.

Goodbye. (saying goodbye to someone who is leaving)

안녕히 가세요.
Annyeonghi gaseyo.

Goodbye. (saying goodbye when you're leaving)

안녕히 계세요.
Annyeonghi gyeseyo.

Thank you for the food. (lit. "I'll eat well.")

잘 먹겠습니다.
Jal meokgetseumnida.

I enjoyed the meal. (lit. "I ate well.")

잘 먹었습니다.
Jal meogeotseumnida.

Have a good weekend.

주말 잘 보내세요.
Jumal jal bonaeseyo.

Congratulations.

축하합니다.
Chukahamnida.

I'm sorry, but...

죄송한데요.
Joesonghandeyo.

Excuse me.

실례합니다.
Sillyehamnida.

Excuse me. (to get someone's attention)

저기요.
Jeogiyo.

Um... (hesitating or trying to get attention)

저…….
Jeo…….

Are you there? / Is someone there?

계세요?
Gyeseyo?

Just a moment.

잠깐만요.
Jamkkanmanyo.

Do you have a moment?

잠시 시간 괜찮으세요?
Jamsi sigan gwaenchaneuseyo?

Thank you.

감사합니다.
Gamsahamnida.

Thanks.

고마워요.
Gomawoyo.

It's no big deal. / You're welcome.

아니에요.
Anieyo.

Don't mention it.

별 말씀을요.
Byeol malsseumeuryo.

I'm sorry.

죄송합니디.
Joesonghamnida.

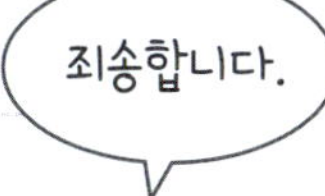

Sorry.

미안해요.
Mianhaeyo.

It's okay. / No problem.

괜찮아요.
Gwaenchanayo.

■ **Welcome.**

어서 오세요.

Eoseo oseyo.

What is this/that?

이건/저건 뭐예요?

Igeon/Jeogeon mwoyeyo?

How much is it?

얼마예요?

Eolmayeyo?

Please show me that.

그거 좀 보여 주세요.

Geugeo jom boyeo juseyo.

Do you have it in another color?

다른 색도 있어요?

Dareun saekdo isseoyo?

I'll take this.

이거 주세요.

Igeo juseyo.

Please ring up my purchase.

계산해 주세요.

Gyesanhae juseyo.

Where is this place?

여기가 어디예요?
Yeogiga eodiyeyo?

How do I get there? Please let me know.

어떻게 가야 해요? 알려 주세요.
Eotteoke gaya haeyo? Allyeo juseyo.

Where is the toilet?

화장실이 어디예요?
Hwajangsiri eodiyeyo?

Where is the nearest convenience store?

가까운 편의점이 어디예요?
Gakkaun pyeonuijeomi eodiyeyo?

Should I go this way?

여기로 가면 돼요?
Yeogiro gamyeon dwaeyo?

Go left.

왼쪽으로 가세요.
Oenjjogeuro gaseyo.

Go right.

오른쪽으로 가세요.
Oreunjjogeuro gaseyo.

Go straight.

쭉 가세요.
Jjuk gaseyo

Is there a bank nearby?

이 근처에 은행이 있어요?
I geuncheo-e eunhaeng-i isseoyo?

Which floor should I go to?

몇 층으로 가면 돼요?
Myeot cheung-euro gamyeon dwaeyo?

How do I get to the other side?

반대쪽에 어떻게 가요?
Bandaejjoge eotteoke gayo?

Take this staircase.

이 계단으로 가세요.
I gyedaneuro gaseyo.

Take the elevator.

엘리베이터를 타세요.
Ellibeiteoreul taseyo.

Please take a look at this map.

이 지도를 좀 봐 주세요.
I jidoreul jom bwa juseyo.

Where do I buy it?

어디에서 사요?
Eodieseo sayo?

What's the name of the store?

가게 이름이 뭐예요?
Gage ireumi mwoyeyo?

When?

언제요?
Eonjeyo?

Why?

왜요?
Waeyo?

What time is it now?

지금 몇 시예요?
Jigeum myeot siyeyo?

What time does it go until?

언제까지 해요?
Eonjekkaji haeyo?

Is it possible?

가능할까요?
Ganeunghalkkayo?

May I ask a favor?

부탁해도 될까요?
Butakaedo doelkkayo?

Of course.

물론이죠.
Mullonijyo.

Sure.

그럼요.
Geureomyo.

Go ahead, speak.

말씀하세요.
Malsseumhaseyo.

It's all right.

괜찮아요.
Gwaenchanayo.

Fine.

좋아요.
Joayo.

I understand.

알겠습니다.
Algetseumnida.

I don't know either.

저도 잘 몰라요.
Jeodo jal mollayo.

That would be difficult for me.

그건 어려워요.
Geugeon eoryeowoyo.

I'm a bit busy right now.

지금 좀 바빠서요.
Jigeum jom bappaseoyo.

No, it's too difficult.

아니요, 힘들어요.
Aniyo, himdeureoyo.

I'm sorry, but I can't.

죄송한데 안 돼요.
Joesonghande an dwaeyo.

I'll have to decline.

거절할게요.
Geojeolhalgeyo.

No, thanks.

괜찮습니다.
Gwaenchansseumnida.

Yes. / No.

네. / 아니요.
Ne. / Aniyo.

You are right.

맞아요.
Majayo.

That's not it.

아니에요.
Anieyo.

Yes, please (give me that).

네, 주세요.
Ne, juseyo.

No, thanks (I don't need that).

아니요, 필요없어요.
Aniyo, piryoeopseoyo.

I'll think about it some more.

생각 좀 해 볼게요.
Saenggak jom hae bolgeyo.

I don't like it.

싫어요.
Sireoyo.

02

On the plane 기내에서

Did you board the plane with an excited heart?
Let's start a conversation on the plane!

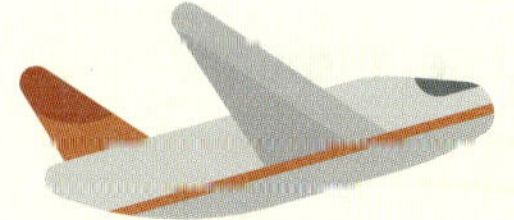

MP3 02-1

■ **Can you show me your boarding pass?**

탑승권을 보여 주시겠습니까?
Tapseunggwoneul boyeo jusigetseumnikka?

Can I board with this?

이거 들고 타도 돼요?
Igeo deulgo tado dwaeyo?

Where is my seat?

제 자리는 어디예요?
Je jarineun eodiyeyo?

Is this my seat?

여기가 제 자리 맞아요?
Yeogiga je jari majayo?

Can you switch seats?

자리를 좀 바꿔 줄 수 있어요?
Jarireul jom bakkwo jul su isseoyo?

I want to put my bag up. Can you help me?

가방을 올리고 싶어요. 좀 도와주세요.
Gabang-eul olligo sipeoyo. Jom dowajuseyo.

Excuse me, I need to get through.

좀 지나갈게요.
Jom jinagalgeyo.

구명조끼	gumyeong jokki	life jacket
기내 수하물	ginae suhamul	carry-on luggage
당기다	danggida	to pull
밀다	milda	to push
비상구	bisanggu	emergency exit
승객	seunggaek	passenger
승무원	seungmuwon	flight attendant
안전 벨트	anjeon belteu	seat belt
이륙하다	iryukada	to take off
좌석	jwaseok	seat
지연	jiyeon	delay
착륙하다	changnyukada	to land
창문	changmun	window
출발	chulbal	departure
통로	tongno	aisle

🎧 MP3 **02-2**

■ **What would you like to have?**

어떤 걸로 드시겠습니까?
Eotteon geollo deusigetseumnikka?

> **Tip**
> 일상 생활에서 '것으로' 대신 '걸로'를 많이 사용해요.

I'll have bibimbap, please.

비빔밥 주세요.
Bibimbap juseyo.

I'll have beef, please.

소고기 주세요.
Sogogi juseyo.

■ **Would you like something to drink?**

음료 드시겠습니까?
Eumnyo deusigetseumnikka?

Coffee/juice/water, please.

커피/주스/생수 주세요.
Keopi/juseu/saengsu juseyo.

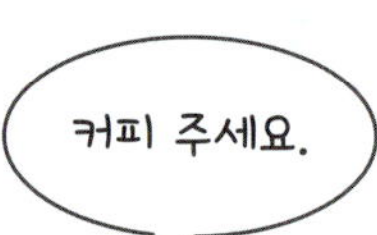

One more coffee/beer, please.

커피 한 잔/맥주 하나 더 주세요.
Keopi han jan/maekju hana deo juseyo.

No, thank you. I'm fine.

아니요, 괜찮아요.
Aniyo, gwaenchanayo.

■ Is there anything else I can help you with?

필요한 것 있으세요?
Piryohan geot isseuseyo?

May I use the lavatory?

화장실 가도 돼요?
Hwajangsil gado dwaeyo?

Could I have some napkins/a blanket/earplugs?

냅킨/담요/귀마개 좀 주세요.
Naepkin/damyo/gwimagae jom juseyo.

My headphones aren't working.

헤드폰이 고장 났어요.
Hedeuponi gojang nasseoyo.

Would it be possible to change my seat?

자리를 바꿀 수 있을까요?
Jarireul bakkul su isseulkkayo?

Could you bring me a snack?

간식을 좀 가져다줄 수 있을까요?
Gansigeul jom gajyeodajul su isseulkkayo?

Could you please clear this away?

이것 좀 치워 주세요.
Igeot jom chiwo juseyo.

🎧 MP3 02-3

■ **Do you need an arrival card?**

입국 카드 필요하세요?
Ipguk kadeu piryohaseyo?

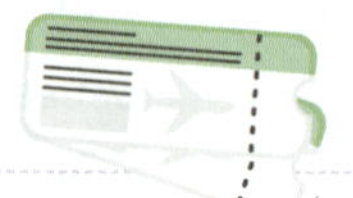

Yes, please give me one.

네, 하나 주세요.
Ne, hana juseyo.

May I borrow a pen?

펜 좀 빌려주세요.
Pen jom billyeojuseyo.

I would like to buy some duty-free items.

면세품을 사고 싶어요.
Myeonsepumeul sago sipeoyo.

I'll take one of these, please.

이거 하나 주세요.
Igeo hana juseyo.

Is this sold out?

혹시 품절되었어요?
Hoksi pumjeoldoe-eosseoyo?

I'll pay with a card.

카드로 계산할게요.
Kadeuro gyesanhalgeyo.

4. 돌발 상황 Emergency situations

Sir/Ma'am, are you feeling any discomfort?

손님, 어디가 불편하세요?
Sonnim, eodiga bulpyeonhaseyo?

I feel a bit sick to my stomach.

속이 좀 안 좋아요.
Sogi jom an joayo.

I feel like vomiting.

토할 것 같아요.
Tohal geot gatayo.

I have motion sickness.

멀미가 나요.
Meolmiga nayo.

Please give me some medicine.

약 좀 주세요.
Yak jom juseyo.

It's a bit chilly. Could I have one more blanket, please?

좀 추운데 담요 하나 더 주세요.
Jom chuunde damyo hana deo juseyo.

The chair is not working. Please help.

등받이가 잘 안 돼요. 도와주세요.
Deungbajiga jal an dwaeyo. Dowajuseyo.

ARRIVAL CARD **(as a foreigner)** 입국 신고서 (외국인용)	※ **Please fill out in Korean or English.** ※ **한글 또는 영어로 작성해 주시기 바랍니다.**	
Family Name / 성	Given Name / 명	☐ Male / 남 ☐ Female / 여
Nationality / 국적	Date of Birth / 생년월일 Y Y Y Y M M D D	Occupation / 직업
Address in Korea / 한국 내 주소 (☎ :) ※ 'Address in Korea' should be filled out in detail. ※ '한국 내 주소'는 반드시 상세하게 작성해 주시기 바랍니다.		
Purpose of visit / 입국 목적 ☐ Tour 관광 ☐ Visit 방문 ☐ Business 상용 ☐ Employment 취업 ☐ Others 기타 ( )		Signature / 서명

03

At the airport 공항에서

Once you get off the plane,
your authentic Korean journey begins!

1. 입국 심사 Immigration inspection

🎧 MP3 03-1

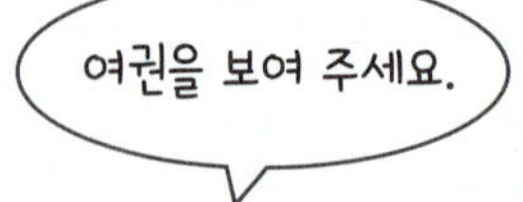

■ **Let me see your passport, please.**

여권을 보여 주세요.
Yeogwoneul boyeo juseyo.

■ **What is the purpose of your visit?**

여행 목적은 무엇입니까?
Yeohaeng mokjeogeun mueosimnikka?

I am going on a tour (business trip/study abroad program/visit).

관광(출장/유학/방문)입니다.
Gwangwang(chuljang/yuhak/bangmun)imnida.

■ **How long do you plan to stay in Korea?**

한국에 얼마나 있을 예정입니까?
Hanguge eolmana isseul yejeong-imnikka?

For three days (a week/a month/six months).

3일(일주일/한 달/6개월) 동안입니다.
Sam il(iljuil/han dal/yuk gaewol) donganimnida.

■ **Where do you plan to stay?**

어디에서 머물 예정입니까?
Eodieseo meomul yejeong-imnikka?

I plan to stay at a guest house.

게스트하우스에서 머물 예정입니다.
Geseuteuhauseueseo meomul yejeongimnida.

한국 입국 절차 Entering Korea: Required Procedures

1. 안내/신고 (Guidance/Declaration):
세관(customs)에 어헹자 휴대품 신고시(traveler's customs declarations)를 주세요.

2. 입국 심사 (Immigration inspection)
여권(passport)과 입국 신고서(entry declaration form)를 보여 주세요. K-ETA 어가(K-ETA approval)를 빋있거나 딘체 비자(group visas)가 있으면 입국 신고서를 쓰지 않아도 돼요. 안전을 위해 입국 심사관(the immigration officer)이 여권의 사진과 얼굴이 같은지 확인하고 몇 가지 질문을 해요.

3. 수하물 찾기 (Baggage claim)

Where can I find my baggage?

짐은 어디에서 찾아요?
Jimeun eodieseo chajayo?

I lost my baggage.

가방을 잃어버렸어요.
Gabang-eul ireobeoryeosseoyo.

My baggage isn't here yet.

제 가방이 아직 안 나왔어요.
Je gabang-i ajik an nawasseoyo.

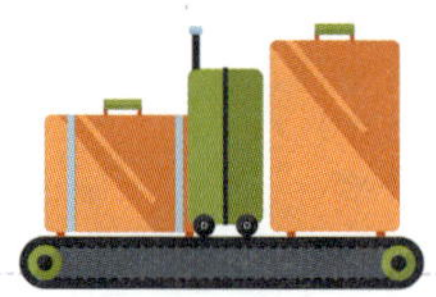

I kept waiting, but my bag isn't here.

계속 기다렸는데 제 가방이 없어요.
Gyesok gidaryeonneunde je gabang-i eopseoyo.

What kind of baggage is it?

어떤 종류의 가방입니까?
Eotteon jongnyuui gabang-imnikka?

It's a blue suitcase.

파란색 여행 가방입니다.
Paransaek yeohaeng gabang-imnida.

If you find it, please contact me at this number.

찾으면 여기로 연락 주세요.
Chajeumyeon yeogiro yeollak juseyo.

■ **Do you have anything to report?**

신고하실 것이 있습니까?
Singohasil geosi itseumnikka?

■ **Do you have alcohol or cigarettes?**

술이나 담배를 가지고 있나요?
Surina dambaereul gajigo innayo?

No, I don't have any.

없습니다.
Eopseumnida.

■ **Please open your suitcase.**

가방을 열어 주세요.
Gabang-eul yeoreo juseyo.

■ **Can you tell me what this is?**

이건 뭐에요?
Igeon mwoyeyo?

It's a gift (perfume/some medicine/a watch).

선물(향수/약/시계)입니다.
Seonmul(hyangsu/yak/sigye)imnida.

It's a laptop/camera.

노트북/카메라입니다.
Noteubuk/Kameraimnida.

🎧 MP3 03-4

How do I get to Seoul?

서울까지 어떻게 가면 돼요?
Seoulkkaji eotteoke gamyeon dwaeyo?

Where can I buy a transportation card?

교통 카드는 어디에서 사요?
Gyotong kadeuneun eodieseo sayo?

Please charge this (transportation card) with 10,000 won.

만 원 충전해 주세요.
Man won chungjeonhae juseyo.

I also want to buy a USIM card.

USIM도 사고 싶어요.
USIMdo sago sipeoyo.

Tip **교통 카드, USIM 구매 방법** How to Purchase Transportation Cards/USIMs

충전식 교통 카드를 사는 방법
편의점이나 공항의 종합 안내 센터(information center), 관광지의 여행 센터(travel center) 등에서 충전식 교통 카드를 살 수 있어요.

USIM을 사는 방법
공항에 있는 통신사 카운터(mobile carrier counter)에 살 수 있어요. 편의점에서도 살 수 있지만 따로 등록해야 사용할 수 있어요.

Where do I catch the airport train?

공항철도는 어디에서 타야 해요?
Gonghangcheoldoneun eodieseo taya haeyo?

Where should I buy a ticket?

승차권은 어디에서 사야 해요?
Seungchagwoneun eodieseo saya haeyo?

You can buy it from the ticket vending machine.

승차권 발매기에서 사면 돼요.
Seungchaqwon balmaegieseo samyeon dwaeyo.

(While showing a note) **Which mode of transportation should I take to get here?**

(메모를 보여 주면서) 여기로 가려면 어떤 것을 타야 해요?
Yeogiro garyeomyeon eotteon geoseul taya haeyo?

Should I take the express train?

직통 열차를 타면 되지요?
Jiktong yeolchareul tamyeon doejiyo?

I want to know the train schedule.

열차 시간표를 알고 싶어요.
Yeolcha siganpyoreul algo sipeoyo.

What time is the last train?

막차는 몇 시에 있어요?
Makchaneun myeot sie isseoyo?

Where do I catch the airport bus?

공항버스는 어디에서 타요?
Gonghangbeoseuneun eodieseo tayo?

■ **Please check this information notice.**

여기 안내문을 확인하세요.
Yeogi annaemuneul hwaginhaseyo.

Where do I purchase a ticket?

승차권은 어디에서 구입해요?
Seungchagwoneun eodieseo guipaeyo?

■ **Use the ticket counter or vending machine.**

매표소나 발매기를 이용하세요.
Maepyosona balmaegireul iyonghaseyo.

How often does the bus come?

버스는 몇 분마다 와요?
Beoseuneun myeot bunmada wayo?

■ **It comes every 40 minutes.**

40분마다 옵니다.
Sasip bunmada omnida.

■ **Please put your luggage here.**

짐은 여기에 넣어 주세요.
Jimeun yeogie neoeo juseyo.

04

Getting around 이동하기

Let's use transportation to get to our destination!
It's more convenient if you download the relevant app in advance!

MP3 04-1

Where do I take the subway to Hongdae Station?

홍대역으로 가는 지하철은 어디에서 타요?

Hongdaeyeogeuro ganeun jihacheoreun eodieseo tayo?

You can go up these stairs.

이 계단으로 올라가면 돼요.

I gyedaneuro ollagamyeon dwaeyo.

How do I buy a ticket? Please tell/show me how.

표는 어떻게 사요? 알려 주세요.

Pyoneun eotteoke sayo? Allyeo juseyo.

How long does it take to get there from here?

여기에서 거기까지 얼마나 걸려요?

Yeogieseo geogikkaji eolmana geollyeoyo?

It takes about an hour.

1시간 정도 걸려요.

Han sigan jeongdo geollyeoyo.

Does this subway go to Hongdae Station?

이 지하철이 홍대역에 가요?

I jihacheori hongdaeyeoge gayo?

No, take it from the opposite side.

아니요, 반대쪽에서 타세요.

Aniyo, bandaejjogeseo taseyo.

Where do I need to transfer?

어디에서 갈아타야 해요?
Eodieseo garataya haeyo?

■ **Transfer at City Hall Station.**

시청역에서 갈아타세요.
Sicheongyeogeseo garataseyo.

Which line should I take?

몇 호선을 타야 해요?
Myeot hoseoneul taya haeyo?

■ **You should take Line 2.**

2호선을 타야 해요.
I hoseoneul taya haeyo.

©이경준

Useful Words

개찰구	gaechalgu	ticket gate
다음 역	da-eum yeok	next stop
매표소	maepyoso	ticket booth
반대쪽	bandaejjok	opposite side
이쪽 / 저쪽	ijjok/jeojjok	this way / that way
환승	hwanseung	transfer
N호선	N hoseon	line N

서울 지하철 100배 즐기기
Enjoying Seoul Subway 100 Times More

서울의 지하철은 주변의 경기도(Gyeonggi-do Province), 인천시(Incheon city)와 연결되어 있어서 수도권 지하철(the metropolitan subway)이라고 불려요. 수도권(metropolitan area)에는 한국 인구(population)의 절반이 살고 있기 때문에, 수도권 지하철은 노선(line)이 굉장히 많고 복잡한 편이에요. 그렇지만 수도권의 여기저기를 연결하고 있어서 지하철로 편리하게 이동할 수 있어요.

지하철과 버스의 요금 시스템(fare system)이 하나로 되어 있어서 버스로 환승할 수 있고, 기본요금(base fare)을 넘으면 5km에 100원만 내면 돼요.

이름은 지하철이지만, 지하철이 땅 위로 지나가는 역도 있어요. 보통 다리와 강 근처의 역들인데, 지하철이 땅 위로 지나갈 때 창밖으로 아름다운 경치를 감상할 수 있어요.

ⓒ한국관광공사 포토코리아–이범수

ⓒ한국관광공사 포토코리아–주민호

일회용 교통 카드 사는 법
How to Buy a Single-Use Transportation Card

1. 사는 방법과 조심해야 하는 내용

지하철역 안에 있는 기계를 사용해서 살 수 있어요. 먼저 기계에서 언어를 선택하고 나서 목적지(detination)를 선택하면 돼요. 그런데 현금(cash)만 사용할 수 있어요. 그리고 지하철을 탈 때만 사용할 수 있기 때문에 버스로 환승할(transfer) 때는 다회용 교통 카드(reusable transportation card)를 구입해야 해요. 버스에서 지하철로 환승하려면 내릴 때 꼭 교통 카드를 찍고 내려야 해요.

2. 보증금을 돌려 받는 방법

보증금 500원은 목적지에서 돌려받을 수 있어요. 지하철 역에 도착한 다음 보증금 환급기(deposit refund machine)에 카드를 넣으면 바로 보증금이 나와요.

Where is the bus stop?

버스 정류장이 어디예요?

Beoseu jeongnyujang-i eodiyeyo?

Does this bus go to Myeongdong?

이 버스 명동까지 가요?

I beoseu myeongdongkkaji gayo?

What time does the bus come?

몇 시에 버스가 있어요?

Myeot sie beoseuga isseoyo?

■ **There's one every 10 minutes.**

10분마다 있어요.

Sip bunmada isseoyo.

How long does it take? Please tell me.

시간이 얼마나 걸려요? 알려 주세요.

Sigani eolmana geollyeoyo? Allyeo juseyo.

How much is the bus fare?

버스비가 얼마예요?

Beoseubiga eolmayeyo?

(Before tapping the transit card) **Driver, for two people, please.**

(교통 카드를 찍기 전에) 기사님, 두 명이요.

Gisanim, du myeong-iyo.

Where are we now?

지금 어디까지 왔어요?
Jigeum eodikkaji wasseoyo?

What time will we arrive?

몇 시쯤 도착해요?
Myeot sijjeum dochakaeyo?

■ **We will arrive in about 30 minutes.**

30분쯤 후에 도착해요.
Samsip bunjjeum hue dochakaeyo.

■ **(Announcement voice when tagging the card while getting off) Disembarking.**

(하차하며 카드를 태그할 때 안내 음성) 하차입니다.
Hachaimnida.

"You need to press the stop button (하차벨) before getting off the bus."

Tip 버스 안내 방송 **Bus Announcements**

한국 버스의 안내 방송은 보통 이런 내용이 나와요.

> 이번 정류장은 OO입니다. 다음 정류장은 OO입니다.
> (This stop is OO. The next stop is OO.)

이번 정류장이 어디인지 버스 앞에 있는 선광판(electronic sign board)에서도 볼 수 있어요. 안내 방송은 영어로도 방송돼요.

Please open the trunk.

트렁크 좀 열어 주세요.
Teureongkeu jom yeoreo juseyo.

Please go to Myeongdong.

명동으로 가 주세요.
Myeongdong-euro ga juseyo.

Please go to this address.

이 주소로 가 주세요.
I jusoro ga juseyo.

How long will it take?

얼마나 걸릴까요?
Eolmana geollilkkayo?

Please turn on/off the air conditioner.

에어컨 좀 켜 주세요/꺼 주세요.
Eeokeon jom kyeo juseyo/kkeo juseyo.

I'm sorry, but please go a bit faster.

죄송하지만 좀 빨리 가 주세요.
Joesonghajiman jom ppalli ga juseyo.

Please stop there.

저기서 세워 주세요.
Jeogiseo sewo juseyo.

기본요금	gibonnyogeum	base fare
빈 차	bin cha	vacant car
사거리	sageori	intersection
신호등	sinhodeung	traffic light
신용 카드	sinyong kadeu	credit card
영수증	yeongsujeung	receipt
예약 중	yeyak jung	reserved
우회전	uhoejeon	right turn
잔돈	jandon	change
좌회전	jwahoejeon	left turn
지름길	jireumgil	shortcut
현금	hyeongeum	cash
횡단보도	hoengdanbodo	crosswalk

Tip **택시 타기** Taking a Taxi

공항이나 기차역 근처에 있는 택시 승강장(taxi stands)을 이용하기니 길에서 손을 뻗어서 택시를 불러도 되지만, 요즘은 어플(apps)을 이용해서 택시를 이용하는 경우가 대부분이에요. 서울시에서 만든 외국인 관광객 전용(exclusively for foreign visitors) 택시 호출 모바일 어플(call taxi mobile app) 'TABA(타바)'로 택시를 이용해 보세요.

I would like to rent a car.

자동차를 빌리고 싶어요.
Jadongchareul billigo sipeoyo.

How many days will you be renting it?

며칠 동안 빌리십니까?
Myeochil dong-an billisimnikka?

I would like to rent it for 3 days starting today.

오늘부터 3일 동안 빌리고 싶어요.
Oneulbuteo sam il dongan billigo sipeoyo.

Do you have an international driver's license?

국제 운전 면허증이 있습니까?
Gukje unjeon myeonheojeung-i itseumnikka?

What kind of car do you want?

어떤 차를 원하세요?
Eotteon chareul wonhaseyo?

I want a regular car/a big car.

보통 차/큰 차를 원해요.
Botong cha/keun cha-reul wonhaeyo.

How much is it per day?

하루에 얼마예요?
Harue eolmayeyo?

Is the insurance cost included?

보험 가격이 포함되어 있어요?
Boheom gagyeogi pohamdoe-eo isseoyo?

How much is the insurance?

보험료는 얼마예요?
Boheomnyoneun eolmayeyo?

How old is the car?

몇 년 된 차예요?
Myeot nyeon doen chayeyo?

■ **It's a new car that came out last year.**

작년에 나온 새 차입니다.
Jangnyeone naon sae chaimnida.

How much fuel is left?

기름은 얼마나 남아 있어요?
Gireumeun eolmana nama isseoyo?

■ **It's full.**

꽉 찬 상태입니다.
Kkwak chan sangtaeimnida.

■ **Please return the car here by 5 PM.**

오후 5시까지 차를 이곳으로 놀려수세요.
Ohu daseot si kkaji chareul igoseuro dollyeojuseyo.

Please fill it up with gasoline/diesel.

휘발유/경유로 가득 채워 주세요.

Hwiballyu/Gyeongyu-ro gadeuk chaewo juseyo.

Please give me 50,000 won worth.

5만 원어치 넣어 주세요.

Oman woneochi neoeo juseyo.

I'd like to use the restroom.

화장실 좀 쓸게요.

Hwajangsil jom sseulgeyo.

How much is an automatic car wash?

자동 세차는 얼마예요?

Jadong sechaneun eolmayeyo?

I'll use a discount coupon.

할인 쿠폰을 사용할게요.

Harin kuponeul sayonghalgeyo.

Tip 셀프 주유소 이용 방법 How to Use a Self-Service Gas Station

셀프 주유소는 운전자(driver)가 직접 기름을 넣는 주유소를 말해요. 대신 가격이 저렴한 편이에요. 기름을 넣는 방법은 기계의 화면에 안내된 대로 진행하면 돼요. 중요한 것은 차에 알맞은 기름이 무엇인지 헷갈리지 않아야 한다는 거예요. 초록색 노즐(nozzle)이 경유(diesel)이고, 노란색 노즐은 휘발유(gasoline)라는 것에 주의하세요.

6. 카센터 Car repair shop

Excuse me, where is a car repair shop?

저기요, 카센터가 어디에 있어요?
Jeogiyo, kasenteoga eodie isseoyo?

The engine won't start.

시동이 안 걸려요.
Sidong-i an geollyeoyo.

The brakes are broken.

브레이크가 고장 났어요.
Beureikeuga gojang nasseoyo.

I have a flat tire.

타이어가 펑크 났어요.
Taieoga peongkeu nasseoyo.

The warning light came on.

경고등에 불이 들어왔어요.
Gyeonggodeung-e buri deureowasseoyo.

I want to change the engine oil.

엔진 오일을 교체하려고요.
Enjin oireul gyocheharyeogoyo.

How much will it cost?

비용이 얼마나 드나요?
Biyong-i eolmana deunayo?

Getting around

05

At the hotel 호텔에서

Let's prepare some phrases you can use at the hotel
to make your stay more comfortable
at your destination!

■ **This is Myeongdong Hotel.**

명동호텔입니다.
Myeongdonghoterimnida.

I would like to book a room.

방을 예약하고 싶어요.
Bang-eul yeyakago sipeoyo.

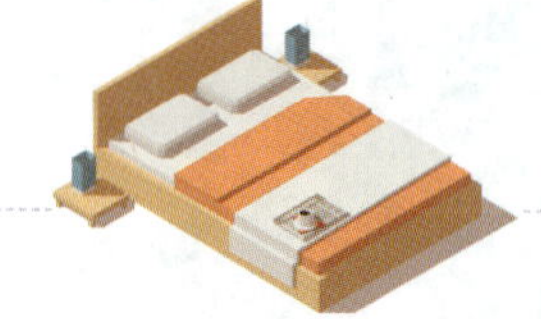

How much is it per night?

1박에 얼마예요?
Il bage eolmayeyo?

Is breakfast included in the price?

조식 포함 가격이에요?
Josik poham gagyeogieyo?

I would like to book for 3 nights and 4 days starting today.

오늘부터 3박 4일 예약할게요.
Oneulbuteo sam bak sa il yeyakalgeyo.

Please give me a room with a single/twin bed.

싱글 베드/트윈 베드 룸으로 주세요.
Singgeul bedeu/teuwin bedeu rumeuro juseyo.

■ **The entire hotel is non-smoking.**

호텔 전체 금연입니다.
Hotel jeonche geumyeonimnida.

Give me a room with a good view/a quiet room, please.

전망 좋은 방/조용한 방으로 주세요.
Jeonmang joeun bang/joyonghan bang-euro juseyo.

What time does check-in start?

체크인은 몇 시부터예요?
Chekeuineun myeot sibuteoyeyo?

Can I leave my luggage before checking in?

체크인 전에 짐을 맡길 수 있어요?
Chekeuin jeone jimeul matgil su issoyo?

What time is check-out?

체크아웃은 몇 시까지예요?
Chekeuauseun myeot sikkajiyeyo?

■ **I'm sorry. All our rooms are fully booked.**

죄송합니다. 방이 다 찼습니다.
Joesonghamnida. Bang-i da chatseumnida.

Tip **한국의 호텔** Hotels in Korea

한국 오텔 중에 한국식 바닥 난방(traditional Korean floor heating)인 온돌(ondol) 객실이 제공되는 경우가 있어요. 온돌방이 있는 호텔이나 한옥 (hanok, traditional Korean house) 체험 호텔을 선택하는 것도 좋은 경험이 될 거예요. 한국 오텔의 조식 뷔페는 보통 안식(Korean cuisine), 양식(Western cuisine)이 있기 때문에 원하는 대로 골라서 먹을 수 있어요.

* 더블 룸 deobeul lum
double room

* 트윈 룸 teuwin lum
twin room

* 욕실 yoksil
bathroom

* 프런트 peureonteu
front desk

객실	gaeksil	room
금고	geumgo	safe
룸 서비스	rum seobiseu	room service
만실	mansil	no vacancy
모닝콜	moningkol	wake-up call
방 번호	bang beonho	room number
비상계단	bisanggyedan	emergency stairs

비상구	bisanggu	emergency exit
비수기	bisugi	off-season
성수기	seongsugi	peak season
시티 뷰	siti byu	city view
신고서	singoseo	registration form
세탁 서비스	setak seobiseu	laundry service
오션 뷰	osyeon byu	ocean view
예약	yeyak	reservation
조식	josik	breakfast
1인실	irinsil	room for one
2인실	iinsil	room for two
체크아웃	chekeuaut	check-out
체크인	chekeuin	check-in

At the hotel

I'd like to check in, please.

체크인하려고 해요.
Chekeuinharyeogo haeyo.

■ I'm sorry, but check-in begins at 3 PM.

죄송하지만 체크인은 오후 3시부터 가능합니다.
Joesonghajiman chekeuineun ohu se sibuteo ganeunghamnida.

Could I store my luggage here before checking in?

짐을 먼저 보관할 수 있을까요?
Jimeul meonjeo bogwanhal su isseulkkayo?

■ Of course, we can do that.

물론 가능합니다.
Mullon ganeunghamnida.

I have a reservation under "Smith."

예약한 스미스입니다.
Yeyakan seumiseuimnida.

■ Please show me your ID.

신분증을 보여 주세요.
Sinbunjeung-eul boyeo juseyo.

■ You've reserved a room with a double bed and a city view.

시티 뷰, 더블베드 룸으로 예약하셨네요.
Siti byu, deobeulbedeu rumeuro yeyakasyeonneyo.

Yes, but I'd like to change to a room with a twin bed.

네, 그런데 트윈베드 룸으로 바꾸고 싶어요.
Ne, geureonde teuwinbedeu rumeuro bakkugo sipeoyo.

■ Let me check if there are any rooms available.

남은 방이 있는지 확인해 볼게요.
Nameun bang-i inneunji hwaginhae bolgeyo.

A room on a high floor, please.

고층 방으로 주세요.
Gocheung bang-euro juseyo.

■ Here is the key to room 705.

여기 705호 키가 있습니다.
Yeogi chilbaego ho kiga itseumnida.

국적	gukjeok	nationality
도착 일자	dochak ilja	arrival date
서명	seomyeong	signature
성	seong	last name
생일	saeng-il	date of birth
이름	ireum	first name
주소	juso	address
출발 일자	chulbal ilja	departure date

Here is room 705.

여기 705호인데요.
Yeogi chilbaego hoindeyo.

The hot water isn't working.

뜨거운 물이 안 나와요.
Tteugeoun muri an nawayo.

I need more towels.

수건이 더 필요해요.
Sugeoni deo piryohaeyo.

The light doesn't turn on.

불이 안 켜져요.
Buri an kyeojyeoyo.

The air conditioning isn't working.

에어컨이 안 돼요.
Eeokeoni an dwaeyo.

The next room is too noisy.

옆방이 너무 시끄러워요.
Yeopbang-i neomu sikkeureowoyo.

Can I change my room?

다른 방으로 바꿔 주세요.
Dareun bang-euro bakkwo juseyo.

I'm having a problem. Please send a staff member.

문제가 생겼어요. 직원을 보내 주세요.
Munjega saenggyeosseoyo. Jigwoneul bonae juseyo.

Please wash these clothes.

이 옷을 세탁해 주세요.
I oseul setakae juseyo.

Please iron them as well.

다림질까지 해 주세요.
Darimjilkkaji hae juseyo.

By what time will they be ready?

몇 시까지 돼요?
Myeot sikkaji dwaeyo?

Can you deliver them to my room?

방에 가져다주시나요?
Bang-e gajyeodajusinayo?

Tip | **에어비앤비** Airbnb

에어비앤비는 한국의 집에서 지내고 싶은 사람들에게 맞는 숙소(accomodation)예요. 한국 사람들이 사는 집의 방 하나만 빌려서 같이 생활할 수도 있고, 집 전체를 빌리는 것도 가능해요. 문화 세험(cultural experience)과 교류(cultural exchange)를 둘 다 하고 싶을 때 선택하면 좋아요.

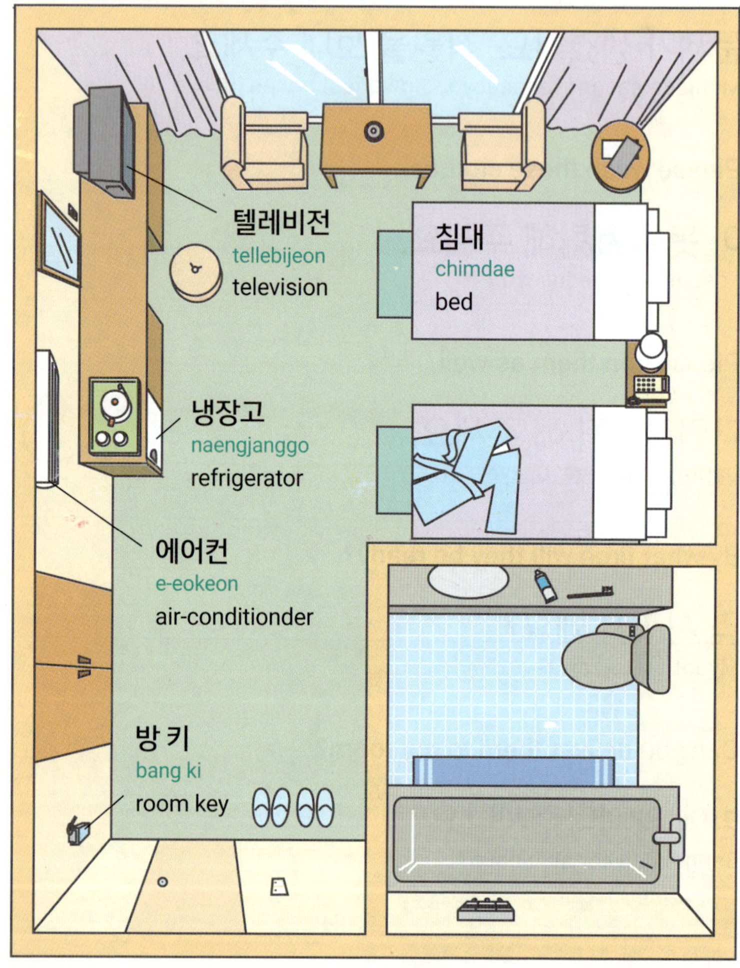

샤워 가운 syawo gaun	shower robe	**베개** begae	pillow
수건 sugeon	towel	**스위치** seuwichi	light switch
슬리퍼 seullipeo	slippers	**욕조** yokjo	bathtub
옷장 otjang	wardrobe	**이불** ibul	blanket

Tip   한국의 전압 Voltage in Korea

한국의 전압(voltage)은 220V이므로 여러 나라와 다를 수 있어요. 미국, 일본, 중국 등 110V를 사용하는 나라에서 온 여행객들은 어댑터(adapters)를 준비해야 해요. 여행 전에 여러 플러그 타입(plug types)을 사용할 수 있는 어댑터나 멀티탭(multi-adapter)을 준비하세요. 만약 이미 여행 중이라면 한국의 마트나 잡화점(household goods store)인 다이소(Daiso)에서 구입하면 돼요. 특히 다이소는 여행 중에 필요한 각종 물건을 저렴한 가격에 구입할 수 있고, 도시 여기저기에 있기 때문에 한 번쯤 방문을 추천해요.

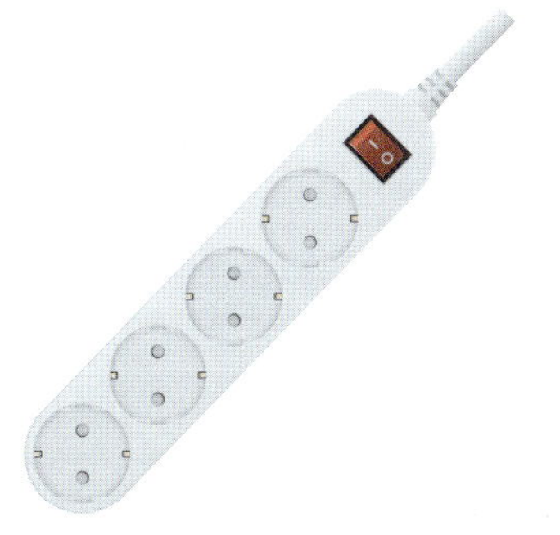

CC BY-LERK

■ **Did you make a reservation?**

예약하셨습니까?
Yeyakasyeotseumnikka?

No, I'll pay for it now.

아니요, 지금 구입할게요.
Aniyo, jigeum guipalgeyo.

■ **How many people are in your party?**

몇 분이십니까?
Myeot bunisimnikka?

It's just me. / There are two of us.

저 혼자예요. / 두 사람이에요.
Jeo honjayeyo. / Du saramieyo.

What are the hours for breakfast service?

조식 시간은 몇 시부터 몇 시까지예요?
Josik siganeun myeot sibuteo myeot sikkajiyeyo?

■ **From 7 AM to 10 AM.**

7시부터 10시까지입니다.
Ilgop sibuteo yeol sikkajiimnida.

Please seat us by the window.

창가 자리로 주세요.
Changga jariro juseyo.

■ **What would you like to drink?**

음료는 무엇으로 하시겠어요?
Eumnyoneun mueoseuro hasigesseoyo?

Coffee/tea, please.

커피/차 주세요.
Keopi/cha juseyo.

Could I have one more cup of coffee, please?

여기 커피 한 잔 더 주세요.
Yeogi keopi han jan deo juseyo.

For dessert, please bring me some ice cream.

디저트는 아이스크림으로 주세요.
Dijeoteuneun aiseukeurimeuro juseyo.

> **Tip** **호텔에서 즐거운 아침식사를 Have a Pleasant Breakfast at the Hotel**
>
> 
>
> 한국 호텔은 보통 오전 6시에서 10시 사이에 호텔 안 식당에서 먹을 수 있어요. 한식 메뉴와 양식 메뉴가 모두 준비되어 있고 자유롭게 원하는 메뉴를 선택하는 뷔페식(buffet-style)이 많아요. 한식 메뉴는 밥과 국, 반찬, 김치 등이 있고, 양식 메뉴는 계란 요리, 베이컨과 소시지, 토스트, 시리얼, 유제품(dairy products), 과일과 샐러드 등이 있어요. 그리고 커피와 차, 주스, 물과 같은 음료도 준비되이 있이요.

Is there a shuttle bus to the airport?

공항까지 가는 셔틀 버스가 있어요?
Gonghangkkaji ganeun syeoteul beoseuga isseoyo?

Could you call a taxi to the airport for me?

공항까지 가는 택시를 불러 줄 수 있어요?
Gonghangkkaji ganeun taeksireul bulleo jul su isseoyo?

Which floor is the hotel swimming pool on?

호텔 수영장은 몇 층에 있어요?
Hotel suyeongjang-eun myeot cheung-e isseoyo?

I left my key in the room. What should I do?

키를 방에 두고 나왔어요. 어떻게 해요?
Kireul bang-e dugo nawasseoyo. Eotteoke haeyo?

Please lend me an umbrella.

우산을 좀 빌려주세요.
Usaneul jom billyeojuseyo.

Please store my valuables.

귀중품을 보관해 주세요.
Gwijungpumeul bogwanhae juseyo.

Can I receive a package delivery at the hotel?

호텔로 택배를 받아도 될까요?
Hotello taekbaereul badado doelkkayo?

Is the spa free to use?

스파 이용은 무료예요?
Seupa iyong-eun muryoyeyo?

How much does it cost?

비용이 어떻게 돼요?
Biyong-i eotteoke dwaeyo?

Is there a discount for hotel guests?

숙박 고객 할인이 있어요?
Sukbak gogaek harini isseoyo?

I want to use the gym.

헬스장을 이용하고 싶어요.
Helseujang-eul iyonghago sipeoyo.

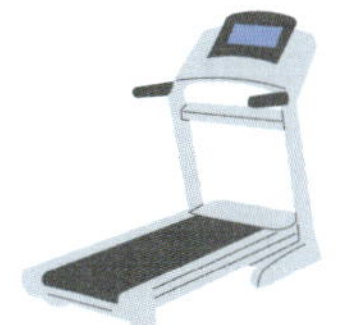

Can I rent workout clothes?

운동복을 빌릴 수 있어요?
Undongbogeul billil su isseoyo?

Can I use a locker?

사물함을 사용할 수 있어요?
Samulhameul sayonghal su isseoyo?

Is there a public computer available?

공용 컴퓨터가 있을까요?
Gongyong keompyuteoga isseulkkayo?

Can I check out a bit later?

좀 늦게 체크아웃할 수 있어요?
Jom neutge chekeuautal su isseoyo?

I'd like to extend my stay for one more day.

숙박을 하루 더 연장하고 싶어요.
Sukbageul haru deo yeonjanghago sipeoyo.

I'd like to check out.

체크아웃 할게요.
Chekeuaut halgeyo.

Could I store my luggage?

짐을 좀 맡길 수 있을까요?
Jimeul jom matgil su isseulkkayo?

■ **How would you like to pay for the additional charges?**

추가 결제는 무엇으로 하시겠습니까?
Chuga gyeoljeneun mueoseuro hasigetseumnikka?

I'll pay by card/cash.

카드로/현금으로 할게요.
Kadeuro/Hyeongeumeuro halgeyo.

Please show me the payment details.

결제 내용을 보여 주세요.
Gyeolje naeyong-eul boyeo juseyo.

I didn't drink from the minibar.

냉장고의 음료수는 안 마셨어요.
Naengjanggoui eumnyosuneun an masyeosseoyo.

I didn't order room service.

룸 서비스 안 시켰어요.
Rum seobiseu an sikyeosseoyo.

■ **Was any part of your stay dissatisfactory?**

이용에 불편한 점은 없으셨습니까?
Iyong-e bulpyeonhan jeomeun eopseusyeotseumnikka?

No, everything was comfortable.

네, 편안했어요.
Ne, pyeonanhaesseoyo.

| Tip | **한국의 모텔 이용하기** Using Motels in Korea |

한국의 모텔은 비교적 저렴한 가격으로 숙박할 수 있는 곳으로, 요즘에는 테마 모텔(theme motel)이 인기를 끌고 있어요. 테마 모텔은 독특한 인테리어 (unique interiors)와 컨셉(concepts)으로 꾸며져 있기 때문에 특별한 날이나 기념일(anniversaries)에 방문하는 경우가 많아요. 스파 욕조(spa tub), 게임기, 노래방 시설 등 다양한 부가 서비스(additional services)를 제공하는 곳들도 많아서 특별한 경험을 할 수 있어요.

06

Eating out 식사하기

When it comes to travel, food is indispensable!

Let's explore some of Korea's representative dishes and restaurants.

■ **Welcome. How many people?**

어서 오세요. 몇 분이세요?
Eoseo oseyo. Myeot buniseyo?

■ **There are no available tables right now so you'll have to wait.**

자리가 없어서 기다리셔야 해요.
Jariga eopseoseo gidarisyeoya haeyo.

How long do we have to wait?

얼마나 기다려야 해요?
Eolmana gidaryeoya haeyo?

■ **It should be about 20 minutes.**

20분 정도 걸릴 것 같습니다.
Isip bun jeongdo geollil geot gatseumnida.

■ **Please leave your name and contact information here.**

여기에 성함이랑 연락처 남겨 주세요.
Yeogie seonghamirang yeollakcheo namgyeo juseyo.

■ **You'll receive a text message when it's your turn.**

순서가 되면 문자가 갈 거예요.
Sunseoga doemyeon munjaga gal geoyeyo.

■ **Sorry, but this is the only table available right now.**

죄송하지만, 지금은 이 자리밖에 없습니다.
Joesonghajiman, jigeumeun i jaribakke eopseumnida.

■ **We'll move you as soon as another one is available.**

다른 자리가 나는 대로 바꿔 드리겠습니다.
Dareun jariga naneun daero bakkwo deurigetseumnida.

■ **I'll show you to your table.**

자리를 안내해 드릴게요.
Jarireul annaehae deurilgeyo.

■ **Would you like to order?**

주문하시겠습니까?
Jumunhasigetseumnikka?

What dish do you recommend?

추천 메뉴 있을까요?
Chucheon menyu isseulkkayo?

What is your signature dish?

대표 메뉴가 뭐예요?
Daepyo menyuga mwoyeyo?

(Pointing to the menu) I'll have this and this.

(메뉴판을 가리키며) 이거랑 이거 주세요.
(menyupaneul garikimyeo) Igeorang igeo juseyo.

Please give us the set for two.

2인 세트로 주세요.
I in seteuro juseyo.

Let's visit 맛집 in Korea!

©본죽 홈페이지

본죽 Bonjuk

죽 전문점으로 여러 가지 종류의 죽을 판매하는 식당이에요. 최근에는 비빔밥과 도시락도 같이 파는 곳이 많아요.

©한솔도시락 홈페이지

한솔도시락 Hansot Dosirak

도시락 전문점으로, 다양한 메뉴의 음식을 저렴한 가격으로 간편하게 먹을 수 있다는 특징이 있어요.

©고봉민김밥인 홈페이지

고봉민김밥인 Gobongmin Gimbapin

한국에서 인기 있는 김밥 전문점 중 하나로, 여러 종류의 김밥과 함께 떡볶이, 분식, 한식 등 다양한 음식을 판매하고 있어요.

©명륜진사갈비 홈페이지

명륜진사갈비 Myeongnyun Jinsa Galbi

무한 리필(all-you-can-eat) 돼지갈비 전문점으로 셀프 바(self-serve bar)에 있는 반찬과 공기밥(steamed rice), 음료 모두 식사 가격에 포함되어 있다는 특징이 있어요.

ⓒ놀부부대찌개 홈페이지

놀부부대찌개 Nolbu Budae Jjigae

한국의 대표적인 부대찌개 전문점으로, 많은 재료와 맛있게 매운 국물이 특징이에요. 부대찌개는 스팸, 소시지, 김치, 두부 등 여러 재료를 넣고 끓인 음식을 말해요.

ⓒbbq치킨 홈페이지

BBQ치킨 BBQ Chicken

한국에서 가장 유명한 치킨 브랜드로, 황금올리브치킨이 대표적인 메뉴예요. 보통 음료와 술도 함께 팔고 있어요.

ⓒ유가네닭갈비

유가네닭갈비 Yugane Dakgalbi

대표적인 닭갈비 전문점으로 철판(iron plate)에 닭갈비와 밥을 같이 볶아서 만든 메뉴가 특히 인기가 많아요. 비교적 저렴한 가격에 밥과 고기, 야채까지 먹을 수 있다는 장점이 있어요.

 Tip

맛집(matjip)은 맛있는 집이라는 뜻으로, 맛있는 음식으로 유명한 식당을 의미하는 단어예요.

한국의 음식점이나 카페에서는 키오스크(kiosk)를 이용해 직접 주문하고 계산할 수 있는 곳이 많아요. 키오스크에서 매장(dine-in)에서 먹을지, 포장(takeout)할지를 선택한 후 메뉴를 고르고, 카드나 휴대폰 페이로 결제할 수 있어요.

Excuse me. I'd like to order.

여기요. 주문할게요.
Yeogiyo. Jumunhalgeyo.

> **Tip**
> 가게에서 사람을 부를 때 보통 '여기요', '저기요' 또는 '사장님(owner)'이라고 불러요.

■ **Would you like to order?**

주문하시겠습니까?
Jumunhasigetseumnikka?

I'll order in a bit.

조금 이따 할게요.
Jogeum itta halgeyo.

Can I change my order?

주문을 바꿀 수 있을까요?
Jumuneul bakkul su isseulkkayo?

I'd like to place an additional order.

추가 주문 할게요.
Chuga jumunhalgeyo.

This isn't what I ordered.

이건 제가 주문한 게 아니에요.
Igeon jega jumunhan ge anieyo.

■ **Can I clear these plates for you?**

접시 치워 드릴까요?
Jeopsi chiwo deurilkkayo?

No, I'm still eating.

아니요, 아직 먹고 있어요.

Aniyo, ajik meokgo isseoyo.

Yes, please clear it.

네, 치워 주세요.

Ne, chiwo juseyo.

Please give me more side dishes.

반찬 좀 더 주세요.

Banchan jom deo juseyo.

Water is self-serve.

물은 셀프입니다.

Mureun selpeuimnida.

Tip **물은 셀프** Water is self-serve.

한국의 식당에서 "물은 셀프"라는 말을 쉽게 들을 수 있어요. 이 말은 물을 직접 가져와서 먹으라는 의미예요. 비슷하게 "반찬은 셀프 바를 이용해 주세요." 라는 말도 직접 반찬을 가져와서 먹으면 된다는 의미예요. 물이나 반찬을 직접 가져와서 먹으면 되는지 궁금하다면 "물은 셀프예요?" 또는 "반찬은 셀프예요?"라고 물어보세요.

🎧 MP3 06-3

Please bring the bill.

계산해 주세요.
Gyesanhae juseyo.

Where do I pay?

계산은 어디서 하면 돼요?
Gyesaneun eodiseo hamyeon dwaeyo?

Do you accept cards?

카드도 돼요?
Kadeudo dwaeyo?

■ **Yes, please sign here.**

네, 여기 서명해 주세요.
Ne, yeogi seomyeonghae juseyo.

Please give me the receipt.

영수증을 주세요.
Yeongsujeung-eul juseyo.

Please put it all on one bill.

다 같이 계산해 주세요.
Da gachi gyesanhae juseyo.

Please split the bill.

따로 계산해 주세요.
Ttaro gyesanhae juseyo.

I think there's a mistake with the bill.

계산이 잘못된 것 같아요.

Gyesani jalmotdoen geot gatayo.

I'll cancel the payment and recalculate it for you.

취소하고 다시 계산해 드릴게요.

Chwisohago dasi gyesanhae deurilgeyo.

Please come again.

다음에 또 오세요.

Da-eume tto oseyo.

수저와 냅킨 등이 테이블 옆 작은 서랍에 들어있는 식탁도 있어요.
There are also dining tables with a small drawer on the side that holds utensils and napkins.

Useful Words

계산서	gyesanseo	bill
메뉴판	menyupan	menu
물티슈	multisyu	wet wipes
숟가락	sutgarak	spoon
젓가락	jeotgarak	chopsticks
앞 접시	ap jeopsi	small plate/bowl
컵	keop	cup
휴지	hyuji	tissue

Excuse me. Can I have the menu?

저기요, 메뉴판 좀 주세요.
Jeogiyo, menyupan jom juseyo.

Does this dish contain meat/eggs?

음식에 고기가/계란이 들어가요?
Eumsige gogiga/gyerani deureogayo?

Do you have vegetarian dishes?

채식 요리가 있어요?
Chaesik yoriga isseoyo?

Two set menus, please.

정식 2인분 주세요.
Jeongsik i inbun juseyo.

I have/haven't tried this dish before.

이 요리는 전에 먹어 봤어요/안 먹어 봤어요.
I yorineun jeone meogeo bwasseoyo/an meogeo bwasseoyo.

Please remove the peanuts.

땅콩은 빼 주세요.
Ttangkong-eun ppae juseyo.

Please make it less spicy.

덜 맵게 해 주세요.
Deol maepge hae juseyo.

☆ Vocabulary for Describing Tastes

고소해요	gosohaeyo	It's nutty/savory. (often used to describe the flavor of sesame oil or roasted grains)
느끼해요	neukkihaeyo	It's oily/greasy.
달아요	darayo	It's sweet.
달콤해요	dalkomhaeyo	It's sweet. (a pleasant sweetness)
담백해요	dambaekaeyo	It's mild. (often used to describe clean, light flavors)
매콤해요	maekomhaeyo	It's slightly spicy.
맛있어요	masisseoyo	It's delicious.
매워요	maewoyo	It's spicy.
비삭해요	basakaeyo	It's crispy.
부드러워요	budeureowoyo	It's smooth/creamy.
비려요	biryeoyo	It's fishy.
써요	sseoyo	It's bitter.
새콤해요	saekomhaeyo	It's tart. (a pleasant sourness)
셔요	syeoyo	It's sour.
짜요	jjayo	It's salty.
촉촉해요	chokchokaeyo	It's moist.

☆ 밥 bap   rice

공깃밥	gonggitbap	bowl of rice
김밥	gimbap	Korean seaweed rice roll
볶음밥	bokkeumbap	fried rice
비빔밥	bibimbap	mixed rice with vegetables

☆ 면 myeon   noodles

국수	guksu	noodles
냉면	naengmyeon	buckwheat noodles

☆ 국 guk   soup

계란국	gyeran-guk	egg soup
떡국	tteokguk	rice cake soup
미역국	miyeokguk	seaweed soup

☆ 찌개 jjigae   stew

김치찌개	kimchijjigae	gimchi stew
된장찌개	doenjangjjigae	soybean paste stew
순두부찌개	sundubujjigae	soft tofu stew

☆ 탕 tang   soup

감자탕	gamjatang	pork bone soup
삼계탕	samgyetang	ginseng chicken soup
설렁탕	seolleongtang	ox bone soup

☆ 고기 gogi　meat

갈비	galbi	ribs
삼겹살	samgyeopsal	pork belly
보쌈	bossam	boiled pork wraps
족발	jokbal	braised pig's feet

☆ 생선 saengseon　fish

생선구이	sangseongui	grilled fish
생선찜	saengseonjjim	steamed fish

> **Tip** 국 vs 찌개 vs 탕
>
> 셋 다 고기, 생선, 채소에 물을 붓고 양념(seasoning)을 넣어 끓인 음식을 말해요.
>
> '국'은 물을 많이 붓고 간을 맞추어(seasoned) 끓인 음식이에요. '찌개'는 뚝배기(earthenware pot)나 작은 냄비(small pot)에 국물(broth)을 적게 넣고 끓인 음식이고 보통 짠맛이 나요. '탕'은 국보다 오래 끓여서 국물이 진한 음식을 말해요.

떡국
Tteokguk
Sliced Rice Cake Soup

김치찌개
Kimchijjigae
Kimchi Stew

삼계탕
Samgyetang
Ginseng Chicken Soup

Do you have a table for four?

네 명인데 자리 있어요?
Ne myeong-inde jari isseoyo?

■ **Yes, I'll show you to your table.**

네, 자리 안내해 드릴게요.
Ne, jari annaehae deurilgeyo.

Where are the spoons and chopsticks?

숟가락이랑 젓가락은 어디에 있어요?
Sutgaragirang jeotgarageun eodie isseoyo?

Is this spicy?

이거 매워요?
Igeo maewoyo?

■ **Yes, it's a bit spicy.**

네, 좀 매워요.
Ne, jom maewoyo.

What do you have that isn't spicy?

안 매운 음식은 뭐가 있어요?
An maeun eumsigeun mwoga isseoyo?

Please give us three servings of pork belly and two servings of pork neck.

삼겹살 3인분, 목살 2인분 주세요.
Samgyeopsal sam inbun, moksal i inbun juseyo.

■ **Here is your order.**

주문하신 음식 나왔습니다.
Jumunhasin eumsik nawatseumnida.

Do you grill the meat for us?

고기를 구워 주나요?
Gogireul guwo junayo?

Is this fully cooked? / Is it ready to eat now?

이거 다 익은 거 맞아요? / 이제 먹어도 되나요?
Igeo da igeun geo majayo? / Ije meogeodo doenayo?

What beverages do you have?

음료수는 어떤 게 있어요?
Eumnyosuneun eotteon ge isseoyo?

Please add one more serving of pork belly.

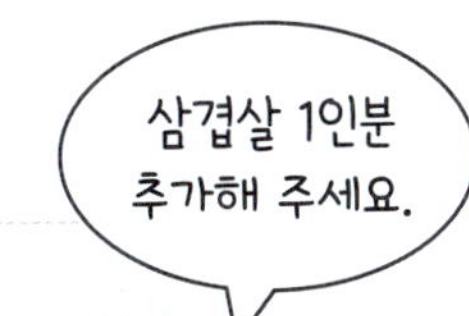

삼겹살 1인분 추가해 주세요.
Samgyeopsal il inbun chugahae juseyo.

Please change the grill.

불판 좀 갈아 주세요.
Bulpan jom gara juseyo.

For after the meal, we'd like cold noodles.

후식으로 냉면 주세요.
Husigeuro naengmyeon juseyo.

■ **Would you like to order?**

주문하시겠습니까?
Jumunhasigetseumnikka?

I'll have an iced coffee, please.

아이스 커피 한 잔 주세요.
Aiseu keopi han jan juseyo.

What are your caffeine-free options?

카페인 없는 메뉴가 뭐예요?
Kapein eomneun menyuga mwoyeyo?

■ **Would you like any dessert?**

디저트는 안 필요하세요?
Dijeoteuneun an piryohaseyo?

No, thank you.

괜찮습니다.
Gwaenchansseumnida.

I'll take it to go. / I'll have it here.

테이크아웃 할게요. / 먹고 갈게요.
Teikeuaut halgeyo. / Meokgo galgeyo.

■ **Your coffee is ready.**

커피 나왔습니다.
Keopi nawatseumnida.

■ **Straws and syrup are over here.**

빨대랑 시럽은 이쪽에 있습니다.
Ppaldaerang sireobeun ijjoge itseumnida.

Can I get a coffee refill?

커피 리필 되나요?
Keopi ripil doenayo?

Can I have a glass of water, please?

물 한 잔 주세요.
Mul han jan juseyo.

Can I have one more fork, please?

포크 하나 더 주세요.
Pokeu hana deo juseyo.

Can I have some more napkins, please?

냅킨 좀 더 주세요.
Naepkin jom deo juseyo.

I ordered a sandwich, but I got a bagel.

샌드위치를 시켰는데 베이글이 니왔어요.
Saendeuwichireul sikyeonneunde beigeuri nawasseoyo.

My order hasn't come out yet.

주문한 게 아직 안 나왔어요.
Jumunhan ge ajik an nawasseoyo.

☆ 커피 keopi   coffee

아메리카노	amerikano	americano
에스프레소	eseupeureso	espresso
카푸치노	kapuchino	cappuccino
라떼	ratte	latte
마키아토	makiato	macchiato
모카	moka	mocha
콜드브루	koldeubeuru	cold brew
플랫 화이트	peullaet hwaiteu	flat white

☆ 차 cha   tea

홍차	hongcha	black tea
녹차	nokcha	green tea
허브차	heobeucha	herbal tea
밀크 티	milkeu ti	milk tea

☆ 기타 음료 gita eumnyo   other beverages

핫 초콜릿	hat chokollit	hot chocolate
스무디	seumudi	smoothie
프라푸치노	peurapuchino	frappuccino
주스	juseu	juice
레모네이드	remoneideu	lemonade

☆ 디저트 dijeoteu　dessert

케이크	keikeu	cake
머핀	meopin	muffin
쿠키	kuki	cookie
크루아상	keuruasang	croissant
파이	pai	pie
브라우니	beurauni	brownie
스콘	seukon	scone
타르트	tareuteu	tart

핫 초콜릿 　　아메리카노 　　마키아토

에스프레소 　　카푸치노 　　라떼

녹차 　　모카 　　플랫 화이드

One serving of tteokbokki, please.

떡볶이 1인분 주세요.
Tteokbokki il inbun juseyo.

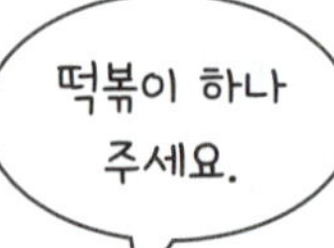

I'd like one some soupy tteokbokki, please.

국물 떡볶이 하나 주세요.
Gungmul tteokbokki hana juseyo.

■ How spicy would you like it?

매운 맛은 어떻게 드릴까요?
Maeun maseun eotteoke deurilkkayo?

Not spicy/medium spicy/very spicy, please.

안 맵게/보통 맵게/아주 맵게 해 주세요.
An maepge/botong maepge/aju maepge hae juseyo.

I'd like some fried snacks and soondae as well.

튀김이랑 순대도 주세요.
Twigimirang sundaedo juseyo.

■ Which fried snacks would you like?

어떤 튀김으로 드릴까요?
Eotteon twigimeuro deurilkkayo?

An assortment, please.

골고루 주세요.
Golgoru juseyo.

Squid and deep-fried eggs, please.

오징어랑 계란 튀김 주세요.
Ojing-eorang gyeran twigim juseyo.

■ Would you like the soondae with intestines?

순대는 내장도 드릴까요?
Sundaeneun naejangdo deurilkkayo?

Yes, please.

네, 주세요.
Ne, juseyo.

No, without intestines, please.

아니요, 내장은 빼 주세요.
Aniyo, naejang-eun ppae juseyo.

Kimbap/rice balls, please.

김밥/주먹밥 주세요.
Gimbap/jumeokbap juseyo.

Please give me fish cakes and dumplings as well.

어묵이랑 만두도 주세요.
Eomugirang mandudo juseyo.

What set menus do you have?

세트 메뉴는 어떤 게 있어요?
Seteu menyuneun eotteon ge isseoyo?

떡볶이
tteokbokki

tteokbokki
(stir-fried rice cakes)

국물떡볶이
gukmul tteokbokki

soupy tteokbokki

순대
sundae

sundae
(Korean sausage)

어묵
eomuk

fish cake

새우튀김
saeu twigim

fried shrimp

야채튀김
yachae twigim

fried vegetables

만두
mandu

dumplings

김밥
gimbap

gimbap
(seaweed rice roll)

주먹밥
jumeokbap

rice balls

닭강정
dakgangjeong

deep-fried and
braised chicken

라볶이
rabokki

stir-fried tteokbokki
and ramyeon

쫄면
jjolmyeon

spicy chewy noodles

■ **Are you looking for something?**

찾으시는 거 있으세요?
Chajeusineun geo isseuseyo?

Where can I find medicine for a headache?

두통약은 어디에 있어요?
Dutongnyageun eodie isseoyo?

Do you have travel adapters?

여행용 어댑터 있어요?
Yeohaengnyong eodaepteo isseoyo?

■ **This item is buy 2, get 1 free.**

이건 2 플러스 1 제품이에요.
Igeon tu peulleoseu won jepumieyo.

Are other flavors also discounted?

다른 맛도 할인 되나요?
Dareun matdo harin doenayo?

■ **Yes, you can mix and match.**

네, 교차 증정 가능합니다.
Ne, gyocha jeungjeong ganeunghamnida.

Please add this to my purchase as well.

이것도 같이 계산해 주세요.
Igeotdo gachi gyesanhae juseyo.

■ **Sorry, we're out of stock right now.**

죄송하지만, 지금 재고가 없어요.
Joesonghajiman, jigeum jaegoga eopseoyo.

Is it possible to charge my phone?

혹시 핸드폰 충전 되나요?
Hokshi haendeupon chungjeon doenayo?

I'm looking for a microwave/ATM.

전자레인지를/ATM을 찾고 있어요.
Jeonjareinjireul/ATMeul chatgo isseoyo.

■ **It's over there on the left.**

저기 왼쪽에 있습니다.
Jeogi oenjjoge itseumnida.

편의점의 다양한 서비스 Various Services of Convenience Stores

간단하게 택배(package)를 보내고 싶을 때 편의점 해외 배송(international shipping service)을 이용해 보세요. 어플(Mobile application)이나 온라인을 이용해 택배를 예약하거나 편의점에 있는 기계를 이용해서 보낼 수 있어요. 그리고 인쇄(printing), 복사(copying) 등 다양한 서비스가 가능한 편의점도 많으니까, 꼭 필요한 서비스가 있을 때 편의점을 이용해 보는 것을 추천해요.

How much is the bung-eoppang, sir/ma'am?

사장님, 붕어빵 얼마예요?
Sajangnim, bung-eoppang eolmayeyo?

It's 1,000 won for three bung-eoppang.

붕어빵 3개에 1,000원입니다.
Bung-eoppang se gae-e cheon wonimnida.

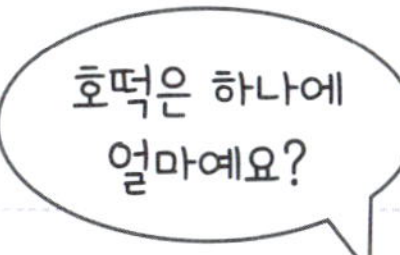

How much is one hotteok?

호떡은 하나에 얼마예요?
Hotteogeun hana-e eolmayeyo?

It's 1,000 won for one.

하나에 1,000원입니다.
Hana-e cheon wonimnida.

Please give me three bungeoppang and two hotteok.

붕어삥 3개랑 호떡 2개 주세요.
Bung-eoppang se gaerang hotteok du gae juseyo.

I've transferred the payment.

계좌 이체했습니다.
Gyejwa ichehaetseumnida.

Thank you.

감사합니다.
Gamsahamnida.

호떡

hotteok

pancake with
brown sugar filling

가래떡

garaetteok

bar rice cake

닭강정

dakgangjeong

deep-fried and
braised chicken

닭꼬치

dakkkochi

chicken skewers

붕어빵

bung-eoppang

fish-shaped bun

떡

tteok

rice cake

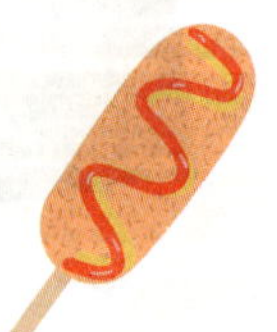

핫도그

hotdog

Korean corn dog

만두

mandu

dumplings

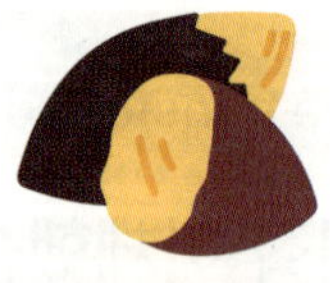

군고구마

gungoguma

roasted sweet potatoes

Half seasoned, half fried, please.

양념 반 후라이드 반 주세요.
Yangnyeom ban huraideu ban juseyo.

One soy sauce chicken, please.

간장 치킨 한 마리 주세요.
Ganjang chikin han mari juseyo.

Please pack two garlic chickens to go.

마늘 치킨 두 마리 포장해 주세요.
Maneul chikin du mari pojanghae juseyo.

■ **Would you like it boneless?**

순살로 드릴까요?
Sunsallo deurilkkayo?

No, with bones, please.

아니요, 뼈 있는 걸로 주세요.
Aniyo, ppyeo inneun geollo juseyo.

One bottle of cola, please.

음료는 콜라 한 병 주세요.
Eumnyoneun kolla han byeong juseyo.

One draft beer, please.

생맥주 한 잔 주세요.
Saengmaekju han jan juseyo.

What side dishes do you have?

사이드 메뉴는 뭐가 있나요?
Saideu menyuneun mwoga innayo?

■ **We have french fries and cheese balls.**

감자 튀김이랑 치즈볼이 있습니다.
Gamja twigimirang chijeubori itseumnida.

What about cheese sticks?

치즈 스틱은요?
Chijeu seutigeunyo?

■ **Sorry, they're all sold out.**

죄송하지만 다 팔렸습니다.
Joesonghajiman da pallyeotseumnida.

☆ **Types of Chicken Dishes**

양념 치킨	yangnyeom chicken	seasoned chicken
후라이드 치킨	huraideu chicken	fried chicken
간장 치킨	ganjang chicken	soy sauce chicken
마늘 치킨	maneul chicken	garlic chicken
허니버터 치킨	heoni beoteo chicken	honey butter chicken
고추 치킨	gochu chicken	spicy chili chicken
파닭	padak	green onion chicken

MP3 06-11

Welcome. Please sit wherever you like.

어서 오세요. 편하신 자리에 앉으세요.
Eoseo oseyo. Pyeonhasin jarie anjeuseyo.

Here's the menu.

메뉴판 여기 있습니다.
Menyupan yeogi itseumnida.

To start, I'll have one bottle of beer, please.

일단 맥주 한 병 주세요.
Ildan maekju han byeong juseyo.

Which makgeolli is the best-selling?

막걸리는 어떤 게 제일 잘 팔려요?
Makgeollineun eotteon ge jeil jal pallyeoyo?

Yuja (citron) makgeolli and chestnut makgeolli are popular.

유자 막걸리랑 밤 막걸리가 인기 있어요.
Yuja makgeollirang bam makgeolliga ingi isseoyo.

I just want a light drink.

가볍게 한 잔 하고 싶은데요.
Gabyeopge han jan hago sipeundeyo.

One bottle of yuja makgeolli, please.

유자 막걸리 한 병 주세요.
Yuja makgeolli han byeong juseyo.

The beer is a bit warm. Can I please have a different one?

맥주가 좀 미지근한데 바꿔 주세요.
Maekjuga jom mijigeunhande bakkwo juseyo.

This beer seems flat.

이 맥주는 김이 빠진 것 같아요.
I maekjuneun gimi ppajin geot gatayo.

Please also bring a cold cup of ice.

시원한 얼음 컵도 주세요.
Siwonhan eoreum keopdo juseyo.

I'd like some soju and soju glasses, please.

소주랑 소주잔도 주세요.
Sojurang soju jando juseyo.

소주의 알코올 도수(alcoholicity)는 16%~17% 정도입니다.

Useful Words

소주	soju	soju	청주	cheongju	cheongju (clear rice wine)
맥주	maekju	beer	매실주	maesilju	maesilju (plum wine)
샴페인	syampein	champagne	백세주	baekseju	baekseju (herbal rice wine)
와인	wain	wine	막걸리	makgeolli	makgeolli (Korean rice wine)
위스키	wiseuki	whiskey	전통주	jeontongju	traditional Korean liquor

■ **What would you like to have with your drinks?**

안주는 무엇으로 하시겠습니까?
Anjuneun mueoseuro hasigetseumnikka?

Please recommend something.

추천해 주세요.
Chucheonhae juseyo.

■ **How about pajeon or tofu with stir-fried kimchi as a side dish for makgeolli?**

막걸리 안주로는 파전이나 두부김치 어떠세요?
Makgeolli anjuroneun pajeonina dubugimchi eotteoseyo?

Then I'll have the pajeon, please.

그럼 파전으로 주세요.
Geureom pajeoneuro juseyo.

Do you have any simple drinking snacks?

간단한 안주는 뭐 있을까요?
Gandanhan anjuneun mwo eopseulkkayo?

■ **We have snacks and peanuts/dry snacks.**

과자와 땅콩이/마른 안주가 있습니다.
Gwajawa ttangkong-i/mareun anjuga itseumnida.

Then I'll have those as well.

그럼 그것도 주세요.
Geureom geugeotdo juseyo.

감자튀김	gamja twigim	french fries
견과류	gyeon-gwaryu	nuts
김치전	kimchi jeon	kimchi pancake
닭발	dakbal	grilled chicken feet
두부김치	dubu kimchi	tofu with stir-fried kimchi
보쌈	bossam	napa wraps with pork
육포	yukpo	beef jerky
족발	jokbal	pig's feet
소시지	sosiji	sausage
치즈스틱	chijeu seutik	cheese sticks
파전	pajeon	green onion pancake

감자튀김

닭발

보쌈

김치전 / 파전

How does it taste?

맛이 어때요?

Masi eottaeyo?

It's a bit bitter.

약간 써요.

Yakgan sseoyo.

It's very delicious.

아주 맛있어요.

Aju masisseoyo.

It seems a bit strong.

좀 독한 것 같아요.

Jom dokan geot gatayo.

It's perfect for my taste.

제 입맛에 딱이에요.

Je immase ttagieyo.

Do you handle alcohol well?

술을 잘 드시는 편이에요?

Sureul jal deusineun pyeonieyo?

Yes, I have a high tolerance.

네, 술이 센 편이에요.

Ne, suri sen pyeonieyo.

No, I have a low tolerance.

아니요, 술이 약한 편이에요.
Aniyo, suri yakan pyeonieyo.

I like it, but I can't drink much.

좋아하지만 잘 못 마셔요.
Joahajiman jal mot masyeoyo.

Should we order more drinks?

술 더 시킬까요?
Sul deo sikilkkayo?

Yes, order as much as you want.

네, 먹고 싶은 만큼 시켜요.
Ne, meokgo sipeun mankeum sikyeoyo.

No, I think I might get drunk.

아니요, 취할 것 같아요.
Aniyo, chwihal geot gatayo.

Shall we all have a toast?

다 같이 건배할까요?
Da gachi geonbaehalkkayo?

Cheers!

건배!
Geonbae!

14. 식사를 끝내고 After finishing a meal

Excuse me. Could we get the bill, please?

여기요. 계산서 주세요.
Yeogiyo. Gyesanseo juseyo.

I'll treat you.

제가 한턱낼게요.
Jega hanteongnaelgeyo.

Please put it on this card.

이 카드로 계산해 주세요.
I kadeuro gyesanhae juseyo.

Let's just split the bill.

그냥 더치페이해요.
Geunyang deochipeihaeyo.

That's right. Let's pay separately.

맞아요. 나눠서 내요.
Majayo. Nanwoseo naeyo.

No, I'll treat today.

이니에요. 오늘은 제가 쏠게요.
Anieyo. Oneureun jega ssolgeyo.

Thank you. I'll get it next time.

감사해요. 다음에는 제가 살게요.
Gamsahaeyo. Da-eumeneun jega salgeyo.

Shall we go for a second round?

우리 2차 갈까요?
Uri i cha galkkayo?

How about noraebang for the second round?

2차는 노래방 어때요?
I chaneun noraebang eottaeyo?

I'd like to have one more drink.

저는 한잔 더 하고 싶어요.
Jeoneun hanjan deo hago sipeoyo.

Let's have cocktails at a place with a nice atmosphere.

분위기 있는 데서 칵테일 마셔요.
Bunwigi inneun deseo kakteil masyeoyo.

> **Tip** **제가 한턱낼게요 / 제가 살게요. I'll treat you.**
>
> '한턱내다'는 남에게 푸짐하게(generously) 음식을 대접한다(treat)는 뜻이에요. "내가 한턱낼게."라고 사용해요. 같은 의미로 "내가 쏠게."라고 쓰기도 해요. 나눠서 내는 것은 '더치페이하다'라고 자주 쓰여요.

07

Shopping 쇼핑하기

Let's explore various shops in Korea in detail!
What phrases can we use when shopping?

◼ **Are you looking for something?**

찾으시는 거 있으세요?
Chajeusineun geo isseuseyo?

I'm just browsing.

좀 둘러 볼게요.
Jom dulleo bolgeyo.

Is there anything you recommend?

추천 상품 있을까요?
Chucheon sangpum isseulkkayo?

Could you show me this?

이것 좀 보여 주세요.
Igeot jom boyeo juseyo.

◼ **Please wait a moment.**

잠시만 기다려 주세요.
Jamsiman gidaryeo juseyo.

Do you have this in a larger/smaller size?

더 큰/작은 거 있어요?
Deo keun/jageun geo isseoyo?

Do you have this in another color?

다른 색깔이 있어요?
Dareun saekkkari isseoyo?

How much is this?

이거 얼마예요?
Igeo eolmayeyo?

It's a bit expensive; can I get a discount?

좀 비싼데 할인 되나요?
Jom bissande harin doenayo?

Can I get a discount if I buy more than one?

여러 개 구입하면 할인 되나요?
Yeoreo gae guipamyeon harin doenayo?

Can I exchange or return this?

교환이나 환불 가능해요?
Gyohwanina hwanbul ganeunghaeyo?

Can I try this on?

입어 볼 수 있을까요?
Ibeo bol su isseulkkayo?

Where is the fitting room?

탈의실이 이디예요?
Taruisiri eodiyeyo?

I'm sorry, but could you please bring me a size up?

죄송하시반, 한 사이즈 큰 걸로 갓다주세요.
Joesonghajiman, han saijeu keun geollo gatda juseyo.

가게	gage	store
가격	gagyeok	price
거스름돈	geoseureumdon	change
계산대	gyesandae	cash register
중고 매장	junggo maejang	secondhand store
교환	gyohwan	exchange
균일 가격	gyunil gagyeok	flat price
세일	seil	sale
마트	mateu	mart
매장	maejang	shop
면세점	myeonsejeom	duty-free shop
반품	banpum	return
백화점	baekhwajeom	department store
보증서	bojeungseo	warranty
비매품	bimaepum	not for sale
전시 상품	jeonsi sangpum	display item
색깔	saekkkal	color
서점	seojeom	bookstore
선물 가게	seonmul gage	gift shop
선물 포장	seonmul pojang	gift wrapping
세금 별도	segum byeoldo	tax not included
세금 포함	segum poham	tax included
세일 가격	seil gagyeok	sale price
세일 중	seil jung	on sale
손님	sonnim	customer

슈퍼마켓	supeomaket	supermarket
시장	sijang	market
식료품점	singnyopumjeom	grocery store
신용 카드	sinyong kadeu	credit card
영수증	yeongsujeung	receipt
영업 시간	yeong-eop sigan	store hours
옷 가게	ot gage	clothing store
잔돈	jandon	change
잡화점	japwhajeom	general store
재고	jaego	stock
정가	jeongga	original price
지불하다	jibulhada	to pay
카드 결제	kadeu gyeoljae	pay by credit card
탈의실	taluisil	fitting room
판매 사원	panmae sawon	sales person
품질	pumjil	quality
할인	halin	discount
환불	hwanbul	refund
현금 결제	hyeongeum gyeoljae	pay in cash

I'd like to pay.

계산할게요.
Gyesanhalgeyo.

Where can I pay?

계산은 어디서 하나요?
Gyesaneun eodiseo hanayo?

How much is everything?

모두 얼마예요?
Modu eolmaeyo?

■ **It's 86,000 won.**

86,000원입니다.
Palmanyukcheon wonimnida.

■ **Please sign here.**

여기 서명해 주세요.
Yeogi seomyeonghae juseyo.

Can I have a receipt, please?

영수증 주세요.
Yeongsujeung juseyo.

Please gift wrap this.

선물 포장해 주세요.
Seonmul pojanghae juseyo.

Please wrap each item separately.

각각 포장해 주세요.
Gakkak pojanghae juseyo.

Can I have a bag, please?

봉투 하나 주세요.
Bongtu hana juseyo.

Please put it in a shopping bag.

쇼핑백에 넣어 주세요.
Syopingbaege neoeo juseyo.

■ There's a charge for the bag.

봉투는 유료예요.
Bongtuneun yuryoyeyo.

In that case, just give it to me as it is.

그러면 그냥 주세요.
Geureomyeon geunyang juseyo.

Can you validate my parking, please?

주차권 좀 주세요.
Juchakweon jom juseyo.

Is delivery available?

배달 가능알까요?
Baedal ganeunghalkkayo?

Can I get a tax refund?

세금 환급 받을 수 있나요?
Segum hwangeup badeul su innayo?

■ **Yes, please show me your receipt and passport.**

네, 영수증과 여권을 보여 주세요.
Ne, yeongsujeunggwa yeogwoneul boyeo juseyo.

■ **Only items over 30,000 won are eligible.**

3만 원 이상인 물품만 가능합니다.
Samman won isang-in mulpumman ganeunghamnida.

■ **I'll prepare the refund paperwork for you.**

환급 서류를 작성해 드릴게요.
Hwangeup seoryureul jakseonghae deurilgeyo.

■ **I'll process the refund immediately.**

바로 환급해 드릴게요.
Baro hwangeuphae deurilgeyo.

What is the procedure for getting the refund?

환급 절차는 어떻게 되나요?
Hwangeup jeolchaneun eotteoke doenayo?

■ **You need to take the documents to the airport.**

서류를 가지고 공항에 가시면 됩니다.
Seoryureul gajigo gonghang-e gasimyeon doemnida.

I want to return this.

이거 반품하고 싶어요.
Igeo banpumhago sipeoyo.

Please refund this.

이거 환불해 주세요.
Igeo hwanbulhae juseyo.

Please exchange this for another item.

다른 물건으로 바꿔 주세요.
Dareun mulgeoneuro bakkwo juseyo.

■ **Please show me the receipt.**

영수증을 보여 주세요.
Yeongsujeung-eul boyeo juseyo.

■ **Yes, I'll take care of it for you.**

네, 처리해 드릴게요.
Ne, cheorihae deurilgeyo.

■ **Discounted items are not eligible for exchange or refund.**

할인 상품은 교환이나 환불이 안 됩니다.
Halin sangpumeun gyohwanina hwanbuli an doemnida.

■ **I'm sorry, but this cannot be returned or exchanged.**

죄송하시만 이건 반품/교환이 안 돼요.
Joesonghajiman igeon banpum/gyohwan-i an doeyo.

■ **What are you looking for?**

어떤 것을 찾으세요?
Eotteon geoseul chajuseyo?

I'm looking to buy a cellphone.

휴대폰을 사려고 하는데요.
Hyudaeponeul saryeogo hanundeyo.

Is this the latest model?

이게 가장 최근에 나온 거예요?
Ige gajang choegeune naon geoyeyo?

Can I get service overseas?

해외에서 AS 받을 수 있어요?
Haeoe-eseo AS badeul su isseoyo?

Is this tax-free?

이거 면세 되나요?
Igeo myeonse doenayo?

What features does it have?

기능은 어떤 것들이 있어요?
Gineung-eun eotteon geotdeuri isseoyo?

Is this sold separately?

이건 별도 판매예요?
Igeon byeoldo panmaeyo?

What is included in the price?

가격에 포함되어 있는 건 뭐예요?

Gagyeoge pohamdoe-eo inneun geon mwoyeyo?

What freebies are available?

사은품은 어떤 게 있어요?

Saeunpumeun eotteon ge isseoyo?

Is there a discount if I buy it with a tablet?

태블릿이랑 같이 사면 할인 돼요?

Taebeullisirang gachi samyeon harin dwaeyo?

Please wrap this product.

이 제품으로 포장해 주세요.

I jephumeuro pojanghae juseyo.

Tip | **한국에서 전자제품을 살 때** When Buying Electronics in Korea

전자제품을 살 때 대형 전자제품 매장(large electronics stores)이나 공식 브랜드 스토어(official brand stores) 이용을 추천해요. 다양한 모델(models)을 직접 비교하고 체험해 볼 수 있고, 직원의 추천과 설명을 들을 수 있기 때문이에요. 도시 여기저기에 많이 있어서 쉽게 방문할 수 있어요. 사고 싶은 제품이 정해지면 온라인 판매 사이트(online retail sites)와 가격을 비교하는 것도 좋은 선택이 될 거예요.

Which floor should I go to buy jeans?

청바지를 사려면 몇 층에 가야 해요?
Cheongbajireul saryeomyeon myeot cheung-e gaya haeyo?

What styles are in fashion these days?

요즘 어떤 스타일이 유행해요?
Yojeum eotteon seutairi yuhaenghaeyo?

I'm not sure if this size fits me.

저한테 이 사이즈가 맞는지 모르겠어요.
Jeohante i saijeuga manneunji moreugesseoyo.

This is a bit large for me.

저한테는 좀 크네요.
Jeohanteneun jom keuneyo.

Can you show me a smaller size?

좀 더 작은 사이즈로 보여 주세요.
Jom deo jageun saijeuro boyeo juseyo.

■ **I'm sorry, but that size is out of stock.**

죄송하지만 그 사이즈는 품절입니다.
Joesonghajiman geu saijeuneun pumjeolimnida.

■ **It looks great on you.**

손님한테 아주 잘 어울려요.
Sonnimhante aju jal eoullyeoyo.

It fits well.

잘 맞네요.
Jal manneyo.

It's too long/short.

너무 길어요/짧아요.
Neomu gireoyo/jjalbayo.

I don't like the color/pattern.

색깔이/무늬가 마음에 안 들어요.
Saekkkari/Muniga ma-eume an deureoyo.

Please show me another color/pattern.

다른 색으로/무늬로 보여 주세요.
Dareun saegeuro/muniro boyeo juseyo.

Useful Words

	니트 sweater niteu		블라우스 blouse beullauseu
	셔츠 shirt syeocheu		양말 socks yangmal
	양복 suit yangbok		치마 skirt chima
	코트 coat koteu		바지 pants baji

I'm looking for this book.

이 책을 찾고 있어요.

I chaegeul chatgo isseoyo.

Do you have this book in stock?

이 책의 재고가 있을까요?

I chaegui jaegoga isseulkkayo?

Where are the Korean language books?

한국어 책은 어디에 있어요?

Hangugeo chaegeun eodie isseoyo?

Where do I go to purchase CDs or DVDs?

CD나 DVD를 사려면 어디로 가면 돼요?

CDna DVDreul saryeomyeon eodiro gamyeon dwaeyo?

Where is the bestsellers section?

베스트셀러 코너는 어디에 있어요?

Beseuteuselleo koneoneun eodie isseoyo?

Can I use this gift card?

이 상품권을 사용할 수 있나요?

I sangpumgwoneul sayonghal su innayo?

Can you gift wrap this book for me?

선물할 수 있게 책을 포장해 주세요.

Seonmulhal su itge chaegeul pojanghae juseyo.

만화책	manhwachaek	comic book
문학	munhak	literature
베스트셀러	beseuteuselleo	bestseller
비문학	bimuhak	non-fiction
신간 도서	singan doseo	new arrivals
어린이 책	eorini chaek	children's book
잡지	japji	magazine
장르	jangre	genre
저자	jeoja	author
추리 소설	churi soseol	mystery novel
추천 도서	chucheon doseo	recommended book
출판사	chulpansa	publisher
판타지	pantaji	fantasy

Tip 한국의 대표적인 서점 Representative Bookstores in Korea

한국에서 가장 유명한 서점은 교보문고(Kyobo Book Centre)예요. 교보문고는 온라인(online)과 오프라인 매장(offline store)을 모두 가지고 있고, 전자책, 음반(albums), 기프트(gifts) 등 여러 가지를 판매하고 있어요. 그리고 오프라인 매장을 중심으로 하는 영풍문고(Youngpoong Bookstore)와 중고 책(used books)을 판매하는 알라딘(Aladin)이 유명해요.

🎧 MP3 07-8

Do you have this skincare product? I don't see it.

이 화장품 있어요? 안 보이네요.

I hwajangpum isseoyo? An boineyo.

If you have a similar product, could you show me?

비슷한 제품이 있으면 보여 주세요.

Biseutan jepumi isseumyeon boyeo juseyo.

I have sensitive skin; will it be okay for me?

피부가 민감한데 괜찮을까요?

Pibuga mingamhande gwaenchaneulkkayo?

Can I test it?

테스트해 볼 수 있어요?

Teseuteuhae bol su isseoyo?

Can I get a sample?

샘플을 받을 수 있을까요?

Saempeureul badeul su isseulkkayo?

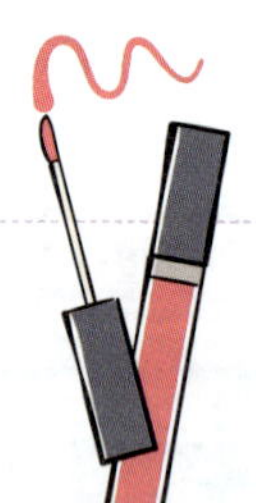

Do you have other color options?

다른 색깔도 있어요?

Dareun saekkkaldo isseoyo?

Will this color suit me?

이 색이 저한테 어울릴까요?

I saegi jeohante eoullilkkayo?

☆ Cosmetics Vocabulary

건성 피부	geonseong pibu	dry skin
로션	rosyeon	lotion
립스틱	ripseutik	lipstick
마스크팩	maseukeupaek	mask pack
민감성 피부	mingamseong pibu	sensitive skin
선크림	seonkeurim	sunscreen
에센스	esenseu	essence
지성 피부	jiseong pibu	oily skin
크림	keurim	cream
클렌저	keullenjeo	cleanser
파운데이션	paundeisyeon	foundation

☆ Colors

	빨강	ppalgang	red
	주황	juhwang	orange
	노랑	norang	yellow
	초록	chorok	green
	파랑	parang	blue
	남색	namsaek	navy
	보라	bora	purple
	갈색	galsaek	brown
	회색	hoesaek	gray
	분홍	bunhong	pink
	검정	geomjeong	black

May I try on these shoes?

이 구두 신어 봐도 될까요?

I gudu sineo bwado doelkkayo?

■ **What is your shoe size?**

발 크기가 어떻게 되세요?

Bal keugiga eotteoke doeseyo?

---

250 mm.

250mm예요.

Ibaegosip milliyeyo.

> **Tip**
> mm(밀리미터 millimiteo)는 줄여서 밀리(milli)라고 하고, 말할 때는 미리(mili)라고 하기도 해요.

These are too big/small for me.

이건 너무 커요/작아요.

Igeon neomu keoyo/jagayo.

They fit well/feel uncomfortable.

잘 맞아요/불편해요.

Jal majayo/bulpyeonhaeyo.

I wish the heels were lower.

굽이 더 낮으면 좋겠어요.

Gubi deo najeumyeon jokesseoyo.

Are these shoes waterproof?

이 신발은 방수가 돼요?

I sinbareun bangsuga dwaeyo?

What material is this bag made of?

이 가방은 어떤 재질로 만들어졌어요?
I gabang-eun eotteon jaejillo mandeureojyeosseoyo?

Do you have a larger size wallet?

좀 더 큰 지갑은 없을까요?
Jom deo keun jigabeun eopseulkkayo?

핸드백	haendeu baek	handbag
배낭	baenang	backpack
지갑	jigap	wallet
동전지갑	dongjeon jigap	purse
벨트	belteu	belt
스카프	seukapeu	scarf
장갑	janggap	gloves
모자	moja	hat
시계	sigye	watch
선글라스	seongeullaseu	sunglasses
우산	usan	umbrella

Can you show me this necklace?

이 목걸이를 보여 주세요.
I mokgeorireul boyeo juseyo.

What material is this ring made of?

이 반지는 어떤 재질로 만들어졌어요?
I banjineun eotteon jaejillo mandeureojyeosseoyo?

Do these earrings come in other colors?

이 귀걸이는 다른 색도 있나요?
I gwigeorineun dareun saekdo innayo?

Is this bracelet adjustable?

이 팔찌는 길이 조절이 가능해요?
I paljjineun giri jojeori ganeunghaeyo?

Is this necklace 14k or 18k?

이 제품은 14k예요, 18K예요?
I jepumeun sipsa keiyeyo, sippal keiyeyo?

Is this ring pure gold?

이 제품은 순금이에요?
I jepumeun sungeumieyo?

Is this bracelet made of silver?

이 팔찌는 은으로 만들어졌어요?
I paljjineun euneuro mandeureojyeosseoyo?

Are these earrings hypoallergenic?

이 귀걸이는 알레르기 방지가 되어 있어요?

I gwigeorineun allereugi bangjiga doe-eo isseoyo?

How much is the set?

세트로 얼마예요?

Seteuro eolmayeyo?

☆ **Vocabulary Related to Accessories**

귀걸이	gwigeori	earrings
목걸이	mokgeori	necklace
반지	banji	ring
발찌	baljji	anklet
브로치	beurochi	brooch
팔찌	paljji	bracelet
헤어밴드	he-eobaendeu	headband
헤어핀	he-eopin	hair pin

I need to get glasses fitted.

안경을 맞추려고 하는데요.

Angyeong-eul matchuryeogo haneundeyo.

I'd like to buy contact lenses.

렌즈를 사려고요.

Renjeureul saryeogoyo.

■ We need to check your vision.

시력을 재야 합니다.

Siryeogeul jaeya hamnida.

■ Can you see clearly?

잘 보이세요?

Jal boiseyo?

Please show me these frames.

테는 이걸로 보여 주세요.

Teneun igeollo boyeo juseyo.

What types of lenses do you have?

알은 어떤 종류가 있어요?

Areun eotteon jongnyuga isseoyo?

■ Try on these glasses.

안경을 한번 껴 보세요.

Angyeong-eul hanbeon kkyeo boseyo.

The prescription is too strong.

도수가 너무 높아요.
Dosuga neomu nopayo.

I can't see well.

잘 안 보여요.
Jal an boyeoyo.

I feel dizzy.

어지러워요.
Eojireowoyo.

Please give me lens cleaning solution too.

렌즈 세척액도 주세요.
Renjeu secheogaekdo juseyo.

■ **I'll give you this for free.**

이건 덤으로 드릴게요.
Igeon deomeuro deurilgeyo.

Tip

덤: A freebie (or freebies). 원래 받아야 하는 것보다 무료로(for free) 조금 더해서 주는 것을 말해요.

Useful Words

렌스 케이스	renjeu keiseu	lens case
안경	angyeong	glasses
안경닦이	angyeongdakki	glasses cleaner
안경테	angyeongte	eyeglass frame
콘택트 렌즈	kontaekteu renjeu	contact lens

I'd like to get a facial.

피부 관리를 받고 싶어요.
Pibu gwallireul batgo sipeoyo.

I'd like an acne treatment.

여드름 관리를 해 주세요.
Yeodeureum gwallireul hae juseyo.

Please shape my nails.

손톱을 다듬어 주세요.
Sontobeul dadeumeo juseyo.

I'd like to get gel nails.

젤 네일을 받고 싶어요.
Jel neireul batgo sipeoyo.

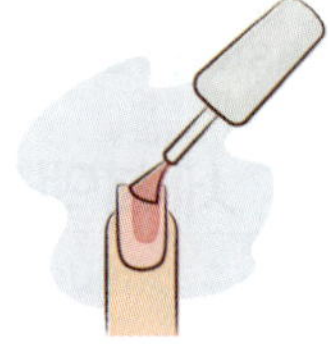

How long will they last?

유지 기간은 얼마나 되나요?
Yuji giganeun eolmana doenayo?

Please recommend a product suitable for me.

저한테 맞는 제품을 추천해 주세요.
Jeohante manneun jepumeul chucheonhae juseyo.

Are there any precautions after the treatment?

관리 후 주의사항이 있어요?
Gwalli hu juuisahang-i isseoyo?

08

Financial services 금융 서비스

If you need to exchange more money or send a package,
try visiting a nearby currency exchange or post office.

■ **Insert your card.**

카드를 넣으세요.
Kadeureul neoeuseyo.

■ **Remove your card.**

카드를 빼세요.
Kadeureul ppaeseyo.

■ **Enter your PIN.**

비밀번호를 입력하세요.
Bimilbeonhoreul imnyeokaseyo.

■ **Select an account.**

거래를 선택하세요.
Georaereul seontaekaseyo.

■ **Enter the amount.**

금액을 입력하세요.
Geumaegeul imnyeokaseyo.

■ **Insufficient funds.**

잔액이 부족합니다.
Janaegi bujokamnida.

■ **The transaction is complete.**

거래가 완료되었습니다.
Georaega wallyodoe-eotseumnida.

☆ Expressions on an ATM Screen

입금 ipgeum	deposit	예금 조회 yegeum johoe	balance inquiry
계좌 송금 gyejwa songgeum	wire transfer	통장 정리 tongjang jeongni	update bankbook
예금 출금 yegeum chulgeum	withdrawal	해외 송금 haeoe songgeum	international transfer
계좌 이체 gyejwa iche	account transfer	신용 카드 sinyong kadeu	credit card
분실 신고 bunsil singo	report lost card	다른 업무 dareun eommu	other transactions

I'd like to exchange currency.

환전하고 싶어요.
Hwanjeonhago sipeoyo.

How much would you like to exchange?

얼마를 환전하고 싶으세요?
Eolmareul hwanjeonhago sipeuseyo?

Please exchange 100 dollars to Korean won.

100달러를 한국 돈으로 환전해 주세요.
Baek dalleoreul hanguk doneuro hwanjeonhae juseyo.

What is the exchange rate?

환율이 어떻게 되나요?
Hwanyuri eotteoke doenayo?

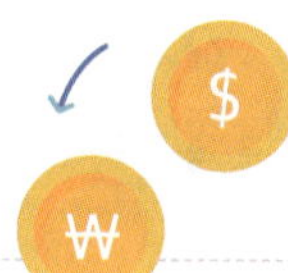

What is the commission fee?

수수료는 얼마인가요?
Susuryoneun eolmaingayo?

How much will I receive after the exchange?

환전하면 얼마를 받게 돼요?
Hwanjeonhamyeon eolmareul batge dwaeyo?

Are there any other currency exchange offices nearby?

이 근처에 다른 환전소가 있어요?
I geuncheoe dareun hwanjeonsoga isseoyo?

I'd like to send a package overseas.

해외로 택배를 보내고 싶어요.
Haeoero taekbaereul bonaego sipeoyo.

I'll send it by EMS/by ship.

EMS/배로 보낼게요.
EMS/bae-ro bonaelgeyo.

How much does it cost?

비용이 얼마예요?
Biyong-i eolmayeyo?

How long will it take to arrive?

도착하는 데 얼마나 걸려요?
Dochakaneun de eolmana geollyeoyo?

■ **What are the contents of the package?**

내용물이 뭐예요?
Naeyongmuri mwoyeyo?

It's books/clothes.

책이에요/옷이에요.
Chaegieyo/osieyo.

■ **What's the approximate value of this item?**

이 물건의 가격은 얼마 정도예요?
I mulgeonui gagyeogeun eolma jeongdoyeyo?

소포	sopo	package / parcel
편지	pyeonji	letter
봉투	bongtu	envelope
우표	upyo	stamp
주소	juso	address
보내는 사람	bonaeneun saram	sender
받는 사람	banneun saram	recipient
배송	baesong	delivery / shipping
등기 우편	deunggi upyeon	registered mail
빠른 우편	ppareun upyeon	express mail
보통 우편	botong upyeon	regular mail
우편번호	upyeonbeonho	postal code / zip code
배송비	baesongbi	shipping fee
국내 배송	gungnae baesong	domestic shipping
해외 배송	haeoe baesong	international shipping

09

Sightseeing 관광하기

What's the travel destination you've been holding in your heart?
Let's go check it out for ourselves.

■ **Where would you like to visit?**

어디를 구경하고 싶으세요?
Eodireul gugyeonghago sipeuseyo?

I'd like to go sightseeing at Suwon Hwaseong Fortress.

수원 화성에 구경 가고 싶은데요.
Suwon hwaseong-e gugyeong gago sipeundeyo.

How can I get there?

어떻게 가면 돼요?
Eotteoke gamyeon dwaeyo?

Where can I buy train/bus tickets to go there?

기차표/버스표는 어디에서 구입할 수 있어요?
Gichapyo/Beoseupyo-neun eodiseo guipal su isseoyo?

How much would it cost?

비용이 얼마나 들까요?
Biyong-i eolmana deulkkayo?

I'd like to go together as a group.

단체로 같이 가고 싶은데요.
Danchero gachi gago sipeundeyo.

Can we make it a day trip?

당일치기로 다녀올 수 있어요?
Dang-ilchigiro danyeool su isseoyo?

What other tourist attractions are nearby?

근처에 다른 관광지는 무엇이 있어요?
Geuncheoe dareun gwangwangjineun mueosi isseoyo?

Is there a package deal available?

패키지 상품이 있을까요?
Paekiji sangpumi isseulkkayo?

How much is it all-inclusive?

모두 포함해서 얼마예요?
Modu pohamhaeseo eolmayeyo?

I'll take that one.

그걸로 할게요.
Geugeollo halgeyo.

Useful Words

가이드	galdeu	guide
경로	gyeongno	route
관광지	gwangwangji	tourist attraction
당일치기	dang-ilchigi	day trip
예약	yeyak	reservation
유적지	yujeokji	historical site
축제	chukje	festival
1빅 2일	il bak i il	two days, one night
2박 3일	i bak sam il	three days, two nights

관광 안내 전화 1330과 함께라면 한국 여행을 더 편하게 할 수 있어요. 여러분의 여행을 도와주는 24시간 서비스가 준비되어 있어요. 여행 일정, 길 찾기, 문제 해결 등이 필요할 때 전화나 메시지를 이용해 보세요.

주요 특징(Key Features):

- 관광 안내(Tourist Information): 교통 시간표에서부터 축제 일정까지 한국 여행을 문제 없이 할 수 있도록 실시간으로(real-time assistance) 도와줘요.

- 다국어 안내(Multilingual Support): 여러 언어로 통역 서비스가 있어서 언어에 문제 없이 이야기할 수 있어요.

- 문제 해결(Problem Resolution): 어떤 문제를 만나더라도 관광 안내 전화가 문제를 해결할 수 있도록 도와줄 거예요.

이용 방법(How to Connect):

- 한국에 있으면 1330으로 전화하고, 해외에서는 82-2-1330라고 전화하세요.
- 무료 어플을 다운로드 받으세요. (와이파이가 필요해요)
- 메시지 어플을 사용하세요.
  서비스는 무료이지만 일반 전화 요금이 적용될 수 있어요.

서비스에 불편한 부분이나 피드백(feedback)을 남기고 싶으면 여기로 연락
하세요.

홈페이지(Website): http://www.touristcomplaint.or.kr
                  http://www.touristcomplaint.or.kr
이메일(Email): tourcom@knto.or.kr

피드백은 바로 처리될 거예요.
의견을 남기면 조사를 한 뒤 해결하고, 결과를 보내 줄 거예요.

Hello. I'd like to go sightseeing.

안녕하세요. 구경하고 싶은데요.
Annyeonghaseyo. Gugyeonghago sipeundeyo.

What's the most famous thing here?

여기에서 무엇이 가장 유명해요?
Yeogieseo mueosi gajang yummeonghaeyo?

What's that building over there?

저건 무슨 건물이에요?
Jeogeon museun geonmurieyo?

Could I get a map?

지도를 받을 수 있을까요?
Jidoreul badeul su isseulkkayo?

Do I need to buy a ticket?

입장권을 사야 해요?
Ipjanggwoneul saya haeyo?

■ **Admission is free.**

입장은 무료입니다.
Ipjang-eun muryoimnida.

What time does it open/close?

몇 시에 문을 열어요/닫아요?
Myeot sie muneul yeoreoyo/dadayo?

Which days is it closed?

쉬는 날이 언제예요?
Swineun nari eonjeyeyo?

Where's the entrance/exit?

입구/출구가 어디예요?
Ipgu/chulgu-ga eodiyeyo?

What's the nearest subway station?

가장 가까운 지하철역이 어디예요?
Gajang gakkaun jihacheollyeogi eodiyeyo?

Is there foreign language commentary available?

외국어 해설이 있어요?
Oegugeo haeseori isseoyo?

Where's the souvenir shop?

기념품 기게가 이디에 있어요?
Ginyeompum gagega eodie isseoyo?

Is there a café or restaurant in the building?

건물에 카페나 식당이 있어요?
Geonmure kapena sikdang-i isseoyo?

Are there any hands-on activities we can do?

체험 활동을 할 수 있어요?
Cheheom hwaldong-eul hal su isseoyo?

MP3 09-3

Is it okay to take photos here?

여기에서 사진을 찍어도 돼요?
Yeogieseo sajineul jjigeodo dwaeyo?

Are there any areas where photography is not allowed?

사진 촬영이 안 되는 곳이 있어요?
Sajin chwaryeong-i an doeneun gosi isseoyo?

Can I use the flash?

플래시를 사용해도 돼요?
Peullaesireul sayonghaedo dwaeyo?

Excuse me, could you take a photo of me?

죄송하지만, 사진 좀 찍어 주세요.
Joesonghajiman, sajin jom jjigeo juseyo.

Where's a good spot for taking photos?

사진 찍기 좋은 장소가 어디예요?
Sajin jjikgi joeun jangsoga eodiyeyo?

Can I use a tripod/selfie stick?

삼각대를/셀카봉을 사용해도 될까요?
Samgakdaereul/Selkabong-eul sayonghaedo doelkkayo?

Are there any must-visit photo spots nearby?

근처에 꼭 가야 할 사진 촬영 장소가 있어요?
Geuncheoe kkok gaya hal sajin chwaryeong jangsoga isseoyo?

I'd like to go to the Hangang River. Which spot is the best?

한강에 가고 싶은데요. 어디가 가장 좋아요?

Hangang-e gago sipeundeyo. Eodiga gajang joayo?

■ **Yeouido Hangang Park is the most popular.**

여의도 한강공원이 가장 인기가 있어요.

Yeouido hanganggongwoni gajang ingiga isseoyo.

■ **What are you going to do at Hangang Park?**

한강공원에서 무엇을 할 거예요?

Hanganggongwoneseo mueoseul hal geoyeyo?

I'm going to rent a bicycle or enjoy a picnic.

자전거를 빌리거나 소풍을 즐길 거예요.

Jajeongeoreul billigeona sopung-eul jeulgil geoyeyo.

I'll spread out a mat and order food to eat.

돗자리를 펴고 음식을 시켜 먹을 거예요.

Dotjarireul pyeogo eumsigeul sikyeo meogeul geoyeyo.

I'd like to try using a picnic set at the Hangang River.

한강에서 피크닉 세트를 이용해 보고 싶이요.

Hangang-eseo pikeunik seteureul iyonghae bogo sipeoyo.

I want to ride a cruise boat.

유람선을 타고 싶어요.

Yuramseoneul tago sipeoyo.

151

🎧 **MP3 09-5**

What's the best way to get to N Seoul Tower?

N서울타워에 어떻게 가는 게 가장 좋아요?
Nseoultawo-e eotteoke ganeun ge gajang joayo?

■ **You can take the cable car from Myeongdong.**

명동에서 케이블카를 타고 가면 돼요.
Myeongdong-eseo keibeulkareul tago gamyeon dwaeyo.

■ **Walking up Namsan Mountain is also nice.**

남산을 걸어서 올라가는 것도 좋아요.
Namsaneul georeoseo ollaganeun geotdo joayo.

What can I do there?

그곳에서 무엇을 할 수 있어요?
Geugoseseo mueoseul hal su isseoyo?

■ **You can enjoy the view of Seoul from the observatory.**

전망대에서 서울 경치를 구경할 수 있어요.
Jeonmangdaeeseo seoul gyeongchireul gugyeonghal su isseoyo.

On TV, I saw couples hanging locks.

TV에서 연인들이 자물쇠 거는 것을 봤어요.
TVeseo yeonindeuri jamulsoe geoneun geoseul bwasseoyo.

(While looking at the view from N Seoul Tower) **The view is so beautiful.**

(N서울타워에서 경치를 보며) 경치가 너무 아름다워요.
Gyeongchiga neomu areumdawoyo.

Itaewon has restaurants from many different countries.

이태원에는 여러 나라 음식점이 있군요.

Itaewoneneun yeoreo nara eumsikjeomi itgunyo.

There are also many stores selling plus-size clothing.

빅 사이즈 옷을 파는 가게도 많네요.

Bik saijeu oseul paneun gagedo manneyo.

I'd like to visit a club or live music venue sometime.

클럽이나 라이브 공연장에 한번 가 보고 싶어요.

Keulleobina raibeu gong-yeonjang-e hanbeon ga bogo sipeoyo.

It's nice that it's close to the subway station.

지하철역이랑 가까워서 좋네요.

Jihacheoryeogirang gakkawoseo jonneyo.

Tip **N서울타워 전망대의 식당들** Restaurants at N Seoul Tower Observatory

N서울타워의 전망대(observatory)에는 서울의 멋진 전망을 즐길 수 있는 여러 레스토랑들이 있어요. 그중에서 가장 높은 곳에 있는 프렌치 레스토랑 (French restaurant) 엔그릴(n Grill)은 야경을 즐기기에 좋고 식당 고객은 전망대를 무료로 이용할 수 있이요. 그리고 한쿡(HANCOOK)은 서울의 경시를 감상하면서 한우구이를 머을 수 있는 식당으로 유명해요.

153

MP3 09-6

I'd like to see a traditional Korean teahouse.

한국의 전통 찻집을 구경하고 싶어요.

Hangugui jeontong chatjibeul gugyeonghago sipeoyo.

How about going to Insadong?

인사동에 가는 게 어때요?

Insadong-e ganeun ge eottaeyo?

You can walk through the alleys and look around the various shops.

골목을 걸으며 여러 가게도 구경할 수 있어요.

Golmogeul georeumyeo yeoreo gagedo gugyeonghal su isseoyo.

I'd like to have a seal made with my name.

제 이름으로 도장을 만들고 싶어요.

Je ireumeuro dojang-eul mandeulgo sipeoyo.

How long will it take? I'll be back in a little while.

시간이 얼마나 걸려요? 좀 있다 올게요.

Sigani eolmana geollyeoyo? Jom itda olgeyo.

It's ready.

다 됐습니다.

Da dwaetseumnida.

It looks great.

너무 멋져요.

Neomu meotjyeoyo.

I'm going to Hongdae. Are there any must-visit places?

홍대에 가려고 해요. 꼭 가야 할 곳이 있어요?
Hongdae-e garyeogo haeyo. Kkok gaya hal gosi isseoyo?

Go to Yeonnam-dong. You can see pretty forest paths and shops.

연남동에 가 보세요. 예쁜 숲길과 가게들을 볼 수 있어요.
Yeonnamdong-e ga boseyo. Yeppeun supgilgwa gagedeureul bol su isseoyo.

I also recommend renting a bike and riding around.

자전거를 빌려서 타는 것도 추천해요.
Jajeongeoreul billyeoseo taneun geotdo chucheonhaeyo.

Seeing an exhibition or play would also be nice.

전시회나 연극을 보는 것도 좋아요.
Jeonsihoena yeongeugeul boneun geotdo joayo.

A club or venue for live music would be fun too.

클럽과 라이브 공연장도 재밌을 거예요.
Keulleopgwa raibeu gongyeonjangdo jaemisseul geoyeyo.

There must be lots of good restaurants and cafes too, right?

맛집이나 카페도 많이 있겠죠?
Matjibina kapedo mani itgetjyo?

Of course. Hongdae can be called a "food heaven."

물론이죠. 홍대는 맛집 천국이라고 할 수 있어요.
Mullonijyo. Hongdaeneun matjip cheongugirago hal su isseoyo.

I want to experience traditional Korean culture.

한국의 전통문화를 경험해 보고 싶어요.
Hangugui jeontongmunhwareul gyeongheomhae bogo sipeoyo.

I'll rent a hanbok and take pictures in it.

한복을 빌려서 입고 사진을 찍을 거예요.
Hanbogeul billyeoseo ipgo sajineul jjigeul geoyeyo.

How often are the traditional ceremonies held?

전통 의식은 몇 시간마다 있어요?
Jeontong uisigeun myeot siganmada isseoyo?

It would be great if I could experience traditional crafts.

전통 공예를 체험할 수 있으면 좋겠어요.
Jeontong gongyereul cheheomhal su isseumyeon jokesseoyo.

I plan to look around the traditional hanok houses in the hanok village.

한옥마을에서 전통 집을 구경하려고 해요.
Hanongmaeureseo jeontong jibeul gugyeongharyeogo haeyo.

Can I have tea there?

그곳에서 차를 마실 수 있어요?
Geugoseseo chareul masil su isseoyo?

It would be amazing to stay overnight in the hanok village.

한옥마을에서 하루 묵으면 최고일 거예요.
Hanongmaeureseo haru mugeumyeon choegoil geoyeyo.

Tip **한복을 입고 고궁에 가자** Let's go to the palace wearing hanboks!

한복을 입고 고궁에 가면 무료로 입장할 수 있는 것을 알고 있어요? 매표소 (ticket office)에 가서 위아래 모두 한복을 입은 것을 확인 받으면 입장 표를 받을 수 있어요. 예약하기 힘든 고궁 야간 개장(evening admission at palaces)도 한복을 입고 가면 무료로 입장할 수 있어요. 낮에도 밤에도 모두 아름다운 고궁에 한복을 입고 가 보세요. 고궁에서 예쁜 사진도 많이 찍을 수 있을 거예요.

경복궁
Gyeongbokgung

덕수궁
Deoksugung

What is the most famous museum in Korea?

한국에서 가장 유명한 박물관이 무엇인가요?
Hangugeseo gajang yumyeonghan bangmulgwani mueosingayo?

■ **The National Museum of Korea is the largest museum.**

국립중앙박물관이 가장 큰 박물관이에요.
Gungnipjungangbangmulgwani gajang keun bangmulgwanieyo.

Can you recommend a museum that's good to visit with young children?

아이들과 가기 좋은 박물관을 추천해 주세요.
Aideulgwa gagi joeun bangmulgwaneul chucheonhae juseyo.

How much is the admission fee for the museum?

박물관 입장료는 얼마예요?
Bangmulgwan ipjangnyoneun eolmayeyo?

Are there audio guides available in foreign languages?

외국어로 된 오디오 안내가 있을까요?
Oegugeoro doen odio annaega isseulkkayo?

Can you buy souvenirs at the museum?

ⓒ한국관광공사 포토코리아-최린

박물관에서 기념품을 살 수 있어요?
Bangmulgwaneseo ginyeompumeul sal su isseoyo?

Are there any restaurants or cafes around here?

이 주변에 식당이나 카페가 있어요?
I jubyeone sikdang-ina kapega isseoyo?

Where should I go during my trip to Busan?

부산 여행에서 어디를 가 보면 좋을까요?
Busan yeohaeng-eseo eodireul ga bomyeon joeulkkayo?

The Busan dialect sounds a bit different.

부산 말은 조금 다르게 들려요.
Busan mareun jogeum dareuge deullyeoyo.

I'd like to learn the Busan dialect.

부산 말을 배워 보고 싶어요.
Busan mareul baewo bogo sipeoyo.

It's my first time visiting Haeundae.

해운대는 처음 와 봐요.
Haeundaeneun cheoeum wa bwayo.

It's nice to be able to walk along the beach.

바닷가를 산책할 수 있어서 좋아요.
Badatgareul sanchaekal su isseoseo joayo.

I was surprised by how tall the nearby buildings are.

근치에 빌딩이 니무 높아서 깜짝 놀랐어요.
Geuncheo-e bilding-i neomu nopaseo kkamjjak nollasseoyo.

It's my first time eating live octopus.

살아 있는 나지는 처음 먹어 봐요.
Sara inneun nakjineun cheoeum meogeo bwayo.

I want to ride the Songdo Cable Car.

송도 케이블카를 타고 싶어요.
Songdo keibeul kareul tago sipeoyo.

They say you can see the entire ocean all at once.

바다를 한눈에 볼 수 있다고 해요.
Badareul hannune bol su itdago haeyo.

부산 광안리해수욕장(Gwangalli Beach in Busan)에서 매년 가을에 열리며 수많은 관광객들이 찾는 인기 행사예요. 부산에서만 볼 수 있는 초대형 불꽃(massive fireworks)과 조명(lights), 음악이 함께 하는 아름다움을 즐길 수 있

어요. 축제는 60분 동안 진행되고, 요금은 무료인데 유료 좌석(paid seating areas)도 있어요. 가을에 부산을 방문할 예정이 있으면, 눈을 즐겁게 해 주는 부산 불꽃 축제를 즐기는 건 어때요?

I'm planning to travel to Jeju Island.

제주도에 여행을 가려고 해요.
Jejudo-e yeohaeng-eul garyeogo haeyo.

Is there anything I should be careful about?

주의해야 할 게 있을까요?
Juuihaeya hal ge isseulkkayo?

The weather changes rapidly, so you should check the forecast carefully.

날씨 변화가 심해서 예보를 잘 봐야 해요.
Nalssi byeonhwaga simhaeseo yeboreul jal bwaya haeyo.

What's the best mode of transportation?

이동 수단은 어떤 게 가장 좋을까요?
Idong sudaneun eotteon ge gajang joeulkkayo?

I recommend using taxis or buses.

택시나 버스 이용을 추천합니다.
Taeksina beoseu iyong-eul chucheonhamnida.

What are some representative foods?

대표 음식은 어떤 게 있어요?
Daepyo eumsigeun eotteon ge isseoyo?

Black pork and seafood dishes are famous.

흑돼지나 해산물 요리가 유명해요.
Heukdwaejina haesanmul yoriga yumyeonghaeyo.

161

I've heard Jeju Island is beautiful in all four seasons.

제주도는 사계절이 다 아름답다면서요? 
Jejudoneun sagyejeori da areumdapdamyeonseoyo?

Yes, the nature is beautiful, so it's great to visit anytime.

네, 자연이 아름다워서 언제 가도 좋아요.
Ne, jayeoni areumdawoseo eonje gado joayo.

When I go to Jeju Island, I'll buy souvenirs related to tangerines.

제주도에 가면 귤 관련 기념품을 사 올 거예요.
Jejudoe gamyeon gyul gwallyeon ginyeompumeul sa ol geoyeyo.

Jeju Island's peanuts and green tea are also famous.

제주도 땅콩이나 녹차도 유명해요.
Jejudo ttangkong-ina nokchado yumyeonghaeyo.

제주의 다양한 박물관 The Various Museums of Jeju

제주도에는 다양한 박물관이 있어서 날씨가 안 좋을 때는 제주도 박물관 투어(tour)를 하는 것도 좋아요. 유리 박물관(Glass Museum), 초콜릿 박물관, 커피 박물관에서부터 해녀 박물관(Haenyeo [women divers] Museum)과 자연사 박물관(Natural History Museum)까지 관심 있는 다양한 주제의 박물관이 있어서 마음대로 고를 수 있어요. 아이들과 함께라면 테디베어뮤지엄(Teddy Bear Museum)도 최고의 선택이에요.

MP3 09-12

I plan to take the KTX from Seoul to Jeonju.

서울에서 KTX를 타고 전주에 가려고 해요.

Seoureseo KTXreul tago jeonjue garyeogo haeyo.

I'm going to stay at accommodations within the hanok village.

한옥마을 안에 있는 숙소에 묵을 거예요.

Hanongmaeul ane inneun suksoe mugeul geoyeyo.

I plan to rent a hanbok and take pictures.

한복을 빌려 입고 사진을 찍으려고요.

Hanbogeul billyeo ipgo sajineul jjigeuryeogoyo.

How do I look? The hanbok really suits me, doesn't it?

저 어때요? 한복이 정말 잘 어울리죠?

Jeo eottaeyo? Hanbogi jeongmal jal eoullijyo?

The fan made of hanji paper is really beautiful. I should buy it.

한지로 만든 부채가 정말 예뻐요. 사야겠어요.

Hanjiro mandeun buchaega jeongmal yeppeoyo. Sayagesseoyo.

This place is famous as a location where a drama was filmed.

여기가 드라마를 촬영한 곳으로 유명해요.

Yeogiga deuramareul chwaryeonghan goseuro yumyeonghaeyo.

It's amazing; I feel like I've stepped into a drama.

드라마 속에 들어온 것 같아서 너무 신기해요.

Deurama soge deureoon geot gataseo neomu singihaeyo.

What are the must-visit places in Gyeongju?

경주에서 꼭 가 봐야 하는 곳이 어디예요?
Gyeongjueseo kkok ga bwaya haneun gosi eodiyeyo?

I'm planning to travel around Gyeongju by bicycle.

자전거를 타고 경주를 여행하려고요.
Jajeongeoreul tago gyeongjureul yeohaengharyeogoyo.

The tourist attractions are clustered together, so getting around is convenient.

관광지가 모여 있어서 이동하기 편하네요.
Gwangwangjiga moyeo isseoseo idonghagi pyeonhaneyo.

I'll take a leisurely walk and then visit the café street.

가볍게 산책하고 카페 거리에 들를 거예요.
Gabyeopge sanchaekago kape georie deulleul geoyeyo.

I've seen many night view photos of Anapji Pond.

안압지의 야경 사진을 많이 봤어요. 
Anapjiui yagyeong sajineul mani bwasseoyo.

It's much more beautiful than what I've seen in pictures.

사진에서 본 것보다 훨씬 더 아름다워요.
Sajineseo bon geotboda hwolssin deo areumdawoyo.

I should buy some Gyeongju bread as a gift for my friend.

경주 빵을 사서 친구한테 선물해야겠어요.
Gyeongju ppang-eul saseo chinguhante seonmulhaeyagesseoyo.

10

Entertainment 즐기기

From clubs to jjimjilbangs (Korean sauna/bathhouses),
let's enjoy leisure in Korea!

Where can I go to see street performances (busking)?

버스킹을 구경하고 싶은데 어디에 가면 돼요?
Beoseuking-eul gugyeonghago sipeunde eodie gamyeon dwaeyo?

■ **You can go to the walking streets in Hongdae.**

홍대 걷고 싶은 거리에 가면 돼요.
Hongdae geotgo sipeun georie gamyeon dwaeyo.

I'd like to know what kinds of performances are available.

어떤 공연이 있는지 알고 싶어요.
Eotteon gongyeoni inneunji algo sipeoyo.

Please show me a schedule of outdoor performances.

야외 공연 일정표를 보여 주세요.
Yaoe gongyeon iljeongpyoreul boyeo juseyo.

What clubs are famous?

클럽은 어디가 유명해요?
Keulleobeun eodiga yumyeonghaeyo?

Please recommend places that are popular with foreigners.

외국인이 많이 가는 곳으로 추천해 주세요.
Oegugini mani ganeun goseuro chucheonhae juseyo.

I'd like to go to hip-hop/jazz/Latin clubs.

힙합/재즈/라틴 클럽에 가 보고 싶어요.
Hipap/Jaejeu/Ratin keulleobe ga bogo sipeoyo.

What would be a good accommodation near the clubs?

클럽 근처 숙소는 어디가 좋을까요?

Keulleop geuncheo suksoneun eodiga joeulkkayo?

How much is the entrance fee for the clubs?

클럽의 입장료는 얼마예요?

Keulleobui ipjangnyoneun eolmayeyo?

늦은 오후나 저녁에 홍대의 걷고 싶은 거리를 걷나 보면 길에 모여 있는 사람들을 쉽게 볼 수 있어요. 노래, 춤, 마술(magic show) 등 다양한 공연이 언제나 열리고 있기 때문이에요. 미리 일정표(schedule)를 확인하고 마음에 드는 공연을 봐도 좋지만, 우연히 본 공연에 마음을 빼앗기는 것도 기분 좋은 경험이 되겠지요. 버스킹을 할 수 있는 공간이 총 4곳이 있으므로, 마음에 드는 공연을 골라서 볼 수 있어요.

■ **Noraebangs are usually located in downtown areas or near universities.**

노래방은 보통 번화가나 대학 주변에 있어요.
Noraebang-eun botong beonhwagana daehak jubyeone isseoyo.

Can I search for songs in multiple languages?

노래 검색은 여러 언어로 가능할까요?
Norae geomsaegeun yeoreo eoneoro ganeunghalkkayo?

I don't know much about songs that have come out recently.

요즘 나온 노래는 잘 몰라요.
Yojeum naon noraeneun jal mollayo.

I'll search for songs I know.

제가 아는 노래를 검색할게요.
Jega aneun noraereul geomsaekalgeyo.

The microphone isn't working well.

마이크가 잘 안 되는데요.
Maikeuga jal an doeneundeyo.

Oh, it works better when I place it a bit farther away.

아, 좀 멀리 놓으니까 잘 되네요.
A, jom meolli noeunikka jal doeneyo.

I feel good because I sang and got 100 points.

노래를 부르고 100점을 받아서 기분이 좋아요.
Noraereul bureugo baek jeomeul badaseo gibuni joayo.

Excuse me, sir/ma'am (lit. owner), **I'd like to add one more hour.**

사장님, 1시간 더 추가하고 싶어요.

Sajangnim, han sigan deo chugahago sipeoyo.

I want to sing just one more song.

한 곡만 더 부르고 싶은데요.

Han gongman deo bureugo sipeundeyo.

How about we stop by a coin noraebang for a bit?

코인 노래방에 잠시 들르면 어때요?

Koin noraebang-e jamsi deulleumyeon eottaeyo?

한국의 노래방은 친구, 가족, 동료들(colleagues)과 함께 일상적으로 방문하는 곳이에요. 거의 모든 동네에 있을 정도이고, 코인 노래방이나 오락실(gaming arcades) 안에 있는 노래방 등 다양한 형태가 있어요. 혼자 혹은 친구와 함께 한국의 노래방에 가서 좋아하는 노래를 불러 보세요.

MP3 10-3

How can I book tickets for the performance?

공연 예매는 어떻게 해요?
Gongyeon yemaeneun eotteoke haeyo?

Is it possible to purchase tickets on-site?

현장 구매 가능할까요?
Hyeonjang gumae ganeunghalkkayo?

I want to book tickets for an evening performance.

저녁 공연을 예매하려고요.
Jeonyeok gongyeoneul yemaeharyeogoyo.

Can I get a student/repeat visitor/credit card discount?

학생/재관람/카드 할인을 받을 수 있을까요?
Haksaeng/jaegwallam/kadeu harineul badeul su isseulkkayo?

How long does the performance last?

공연 시간은 몇 분이에요?
Gongyeon siganeun myeot bunieyo?

■ **Please show me your ID and booking confirmation.**

신분증과 예매 내역서를 보여 주세요.
Sinbunjeunggwa yemae naeyeokseoreul boyeo juseyo.

■ **Please enter 30 minutes before the performance starts.**

공연 시작 30분 전에 입장해 주세요.
Gongyeon sijak samsip bun jeone ipjanghae juseyo.

I'd like to purchase performance merchandise.

공연 MD를 구입하고 싶은데요.
Gongyeon MDreul guipago sipeundeyo.

MD (merchandise products)는 주로 굿즈 (goods)라고 해요.

Am I allowed to bring drinks inside?

음료를 가지고 들어가도 돼요?
Eumnyoreul gajigo deureogado dwaeyo?

Can I leave and re-enter?

나갔다가 다시 들어와도 돼요?
Nagatdaga dasi deureowado dwaeyo?

Useful Words

구역	guyeok	zone
무대	mudae	stage
무용	muyong	dance
뮤지컬	myujikcol	musical
연극	yeongeuk	play
열	yeol	row
예매	yemae	booking / reservation
입석	ipseok	standing
좌석	jwaseok	seat
콘서트	konseoteu	concert
클래식	keullaesik	classical performance
회차	hoecha	number

🎧 MP3 10-4

Can I get two tickets for the 3 PM showing of "Sowon", please?

영화 '소원' 오후 3시 표 두 장 주세요.
Yeonghwa sowon ohu se si pyo du jang juseyo.

What time does the next showing start?

다음 영화는 몇 시에 시작해요?
Da-eum yeonghwaneun myeot sie sijakaeyo?

What kind of seats would you like?

어떤 좌석으로 하시겠습니까?
Eotteon jwaseogeuro hasigetseumnikka?

Could I have seats in the middle please?

중간 좌석으로 부탁드립니다.
Junggan jwaseogeuro butakdeurimnida.

Can I also get a large popcorn and a coke?

큰 사이즈 팝콘이랑 콜라도 하나 주세요.
Keun saijeu papkonirang kollado hana juseyo.

Your movie is in Theater 2.

상영관은 2관입니다.
Sangyeonggwaneun i gwanimnida.

Excuse me, I think you may be in my seat.

죄송한데, 제 자리에 앉으신 것 같아요.
Joesonghande, je jarie anjeusin geot gatayo.

Useful Words

감독	gamdok	director
관객	gwangaek	audience
매점	maejeom	concession stand
매진	maejin	sold out
매표소	maepyoso	box office
상영	sangyeong	play
수상작	susangjak	award winning movie
영화관	yeonghwagwan	movie theater
예고편	yegopyeon	trailer
장르	jangneu	genre
자막	jamak	subtitle
주연	juyeon	leading actor / actress
통로	tongno	aisle
화제작	hwajejak	blockbuster

I want to take a sticker photo.

스티커 사진을 찍으려고 해요.
Seutikeo sajineul jjigeuryeogo haeyo.

I'll wear a cute hat and glasses.

귀여운 모자와 안경을 쓸 거예요.
Gwiyeoun mojawa angyeong-eul sseul geoyeyo.

What pose would be good for taking the photo?

어떤 포즈로 사진을 찍으면 좋을까요?
Eotteon pojeuro sajineul jjigeumyeon joeulkkayo?

They don't give much time, so I need to prepare in advance.

시간을 별로 안 줘서 미리 준비해야 해요.
Siganeul byeollo an jwoseo miri junbihaeya haeyo.

Is it possible to pay by credit card?

신용 카드로 결제 가능해요?
Sinyong kadeuro gyeolje ganeunghaeyo?

Can I set the instructions to English?

안내를 영어로 설정할 수 있을까요?
Annaereul yeong-eoro seoljeonghal su isseulkkayo?

If I don't like it, can I retake it?

마음에 안 들면 다시 찍을 수 있어요?
Ma-eume an deulmyeon dasi jjigeul su isseoyo?

Useful Words

결제 방법	gyeolje bangbeop	payment method
선택	seontaek	select
수량	suryang	quantity
촬영	chwaryeong	taking photos
출력	chullyeok	print
프레임	peureim	frame
필터	pilteo	filter
화면	hwamyeon	screen

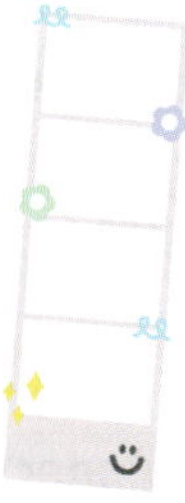

Tip 인생네컷 Insaeng Ne Cut

요즘 한국의 곳곳에서 스티커 사진을 찍을 수 있는 가게를 볼 수 있어요. 가게마다 소품(props), 화면 밝기(screen brightness) 등 작은 차이가 있는네 가상 큰 차이는 프레임(frames)이에요. 스티커 사진 회사들이 연예인(celebrities)이나 애니메이션 회사(animation studios)와 제휴를 맺어(partnering) 관련 프레임을 내놓고 있어요. 좋아하는 연예인이나 캐릭터가 있나면 그 프레임이 있는 스티커 사신 가게를 방분하는 것노 좋은 경험이 될 기예요.

Where is the ski rental shop?

스키 대여 가게는 어디에 있어요?
Seuki daeyeo gageneun eodie isseoyo?

Can I also rent ski suits/helmets?

스키복/헬맷도 빌릴 수 있어요?
Seukibok/Helmaet-do billil su isseoyo?

Where can I buy ski gloves/goggles?

스키 장갑/고글은 어디에서 살 수 있어요?
Seuki janggap/Gogeur-eun eodieseo sal su isseoyo?

I'd like to purchase a season pass.

시즌권을 구입하고 싶어요.
Sijeungwoneul guipago sipeoyo.

Where should I take the beginner's lift?

초보자 리프트는 어디에서 타야 해요?
Choboja ripeuteuneun eodieseo taya haeyo?

How long is the wait time for the lift?

리프트 대기 시간이 얼마나 돼요?
Ripeuteu daegi sigani eolmana dwaeyo?

I want to take a one-on-one ski lesson.

1대 1 스키 강습을 받고 싶어요.
Il dae il suki gangseubeul batgo sipeoyo.

I got hurt in a collision. I need first aid.

부딪혀서 다쳤어요. 응급 처치가 필요해요.

Budichyeoseo dachyeosseoyo. Eunggeup cheochiga piryohaeyo.

I want to go night skiing. What time do you close?

야간 스키를 타고 싶어요. 몇 시에 문을 닫아요?

Yagan seukireul tago sipeoyo. Myeot sie muneul dadayo?

How can I use the lockers?

사물함은 어떻게 이용해요?

Samulhameun eotteoke iyonghaeyo?

Useful Words

강습	gangseup	lesson
고글	gogeul	goggles
리조트	rijoteu	resort
방한복	banghanbok	winter clothing
스노우 보드	seunou bodeu	snow board
스키	seuki	ski
스키복	seukibok	skiwear
스키 부츠	seuki bucheu	ski boots
스키장	seukijang	ski resort
스키 리프트	seuki ripeuteu	ski lift

What are the swimming pool operating hours?

수영장 운영 시간은 언제예요?
Suyeongjang unyeong siganeun eonjeyeyo?

Where can I change my clothes?

어디에서 옷을 갈아입을 수 있어요?
Eodieseo oseul garaibeul su isseoyo?

Is there a lifeguard in the pool area?

수영장 안에 안전 요원이 있어요?
Suyeongjang ane anjeon yowoni isseoyo?

Can I rent a swimsuit?

수영복 빌릴 수 있을까요?
Suyeongbok billil su isseulkkayo?

Can I buy swimming goggles?

물안경을 구입할 수 있을까요?
Murangyeong-eul guipal su isseulkkayo?

How much is the locker rental fee?

사물함 대여 비용은 얼마예요?
Samulham daeyeo biyong-eun eolmayeyo?

How deep is the water?

물 깊이가 얼마나 되나요?
Mul gipiga eolmana doenayo?

Are there swimming lessons available?

수영 강습이 있어요?

Suyeong gangseubi isseoyo?

■ **Please don't run inside the pool area.**

수영장 내에서는 뛰지 마세요.

Suyeongjang nae-eseoneun ttwiji maseyo.

■ **No diving allowed.**

다이빙을 하지 마세요.

Daibing-eul haji maseyo.

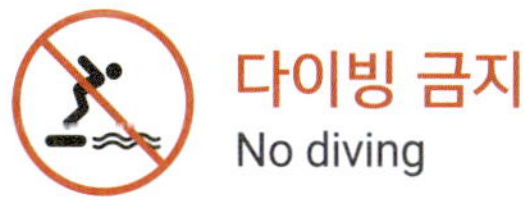

다이빙	daibing	diving
물안경	murangycong	goggles
비키니	bikini	bikini
수영 모자	suyeong moja	swim cap
수영복	suyeongbok	swimsuit
실내 수영상	sillae suyeongjang	indoor pool
안전요원	anjeonyowon	lifeguard
야외 수영장	yaoe suyeongjang	outdoor pool
탈의실	taruisil	changing room
튜브	tyubeu	inner tube

🎧 MP3 10-8

How much is the admission fee?

입장료는 얼마예요?
Ipjangnyoneun eolmayeyo?

Do you have a map of the amusement park?

놀이공원 지도가 있어요?
Norigongwon jidoga isseoyo?

Where is the roller coaster located?

롤러코스터는 어디에 있어요?
Rolleokoseuteoneun eodie isseoyo?

How long is the wait time for the pirate ship ride?

바이킹 대기 시간은 얼마나 돼요?
baiking daegi siganeun eolmana dwaeyo?

Can you recommend rides for children?

어린이를 위한 놀이기구를 추천해 주세요.
Eorinireul wihan norigigureul chucheonhae juseyo.

Am I allowed to bring food into the park?

음식을 가지고 들어가도 되나요?
Eumsigeul gajigo deureogado doenayo?

Can I store my luggage?

짐을 맡길 수 있을까요?
Jimeul matgil su isseulkkayo?

Where is the souvenir shop?

기념품 가게는 어디에 있어요?
Ginyeompum gageneun eodie isseoyo?

What time does the parade start?

퍼레이드는 몇 시에 시작해요?
Peoreideuneun myeot sie sijakaeyo?

Where is the parking lot?

주차장은 어디에 있어요?
Juchajang-eun eodie isseoyo?

Tip **롯데월드와 에버랜드** Lotte World & Everland

ⓒ한국관광공사 포토코리아 김지호

한국의 여러 놀이공원 중 서울 잠실(Jamsil)에 있는 롯데월드(Lotte World)와 경기도 용인(Gyeonggi-do province)에 있는 에버랜드(Everland)가 가장 유명해요. 그중 롯데월드는 도심(city center)에 있어서 이동하기 편하고, 세계에서 가장 큰 실내 놀이공원 중 하나로 기네스북(Guinness Book of World Records)에도 올랐어요. 쇼핑몰, 호텔, 백화점, 아이스링크장(ice rink) 등 다양한 시설이 한 곳에 모여 있어서 한 곳에서 여러 가지를 즐길 수 있어요.

What are the operating hours of the jjimjilbang?

찜질방 영업 시간이 어떻게 되나요?
Jjimjilbang yeong-eop sigani eotteoke doenayo?

Should I take off my shoes here?

여기에서 신발을 벗으면 되나요?
Yeogieseo sinbareul beoseumyeon doenayo?

Where can I get a locker key?

사물함 열쇠는 어디에서 받아요?
Samulham yeolsoeneun eodieseo badayo?

Could I get one more towel, please?

수건을 한 장 더 받을 수 있을까요?
Sugeoneul han jang deo badeul su isseulkkayo?

Where is the red clay room/ice room located?

황토방/얼음방은 어디에 있어요?
Hwangtobang/eoreumbang-eun eodie isseoyo?

Please give me one ramyeon (instant noodles) **and one sikhye** (sweet rice drink)**.**

라면 하나랑 식혜 하나 주세요.
Ramyeon hanarang sikye hana juseyo.

Please give me one roasted egg as well.

구운 계란도 하나 주세요.
Guun gyerando hana juseyo.

I'd like to get a massage.

마사지를 받고 싶어요.
Masajireul batgo sipeoyo.

Can I also get a skin care treatment?

피부 관리도 받을 수 있어요?
Pibu gwallido badeul su isseoyo?

> **Tip** **찜질방 즐기기** The Unique Culture of Korean Jjimjilbangs

한국의 찜질방은 사우나(saunas)와 목욕(bathing)뿐만 아니라, 식사, 마사지, 오락(entertainment) 등 다양한 것을 할 수 있는 곳이 많아요. 그리고 뜨거운 찜질을 하고 나서 식혜와 구운 계란을 먹고, 양머리 수건("sheep head" towel hats)을 만들어 머리에 쓰는 등 독특한(unique) 문화가 있어요. 찜질방에서 사람들은 뜨거운 열으로부터 두피(scalp)를 보호하기 위해서 머리에 수건을 자주 썼는데, 언제인가부터 수건을 양머리 모양으로 만들어서 쓰기 시작하면서 귀엽고 독특한 모양 때문에 인기를 끌게 되었어요. TV 프로그램에서도 종종 양머리 수건을 머리에 쓰고 식혜를 먹는 사람들을 볼 수 있어요. 한국 찜질방에 방문해서 양머리 수건을 쓰고 식혜를 마셔 보는 건 어떨까요?

■ **How would you like your hair done?**

머리를 어떻게 해 드릴까요?
Meorireul eotteoke hae deurilkkayo?

Please cut it short.

짧게 잘라 주세요.
Jjalge jalla juseyo.

Please cut only about 1 cm.

1센치 정도만 잘라 주세요.
Il senchi jeongdoman jalla juseyo.

> **Tip**
>
> 원래는 '센티미터(centimeter)' 의 바른 줄임말(abbreviation) 은 '센티'이지만, 사람들은 cm 를 '센치'라고 발음하는 경우가 많아요.

Just trim it a little while maintaining the style.

스타일은 유지하고 조금만 다듬어 주세요.
Seutaireun yujihago jogeumman dadeumeo juseyo.

I'd like to get a perm.

파마하려고요.
Pamaharyeogoyo.

I want to straighten my hair.

머리를 좀 펴려고요.
Meorireul jom pyeoryeogoyo.

Please dye my hair this color.

이 색으로 염색해 주세요.
I saegeuro yeomsaekae juseyo.

Can you make my hair look like this picture?

이 사진처럼 될까요?
I sajincheoreom doelkkayo?

The perm and cut together come to 200,000 won.

파마랑 커트 해서 모두 200,000원입니다.
Pamarang keoteuhaeseo modu isimman wonimnida.

Do you offer shampooing?

샴푸해 주시나요?
Syampuhae jusinayo?

Would you like me to blow-dry your hair?

드라이 해 드릴까요?
Deurai hae deurilkkayo?

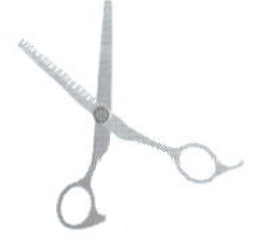

When will it be finished?

인제 끝날까요?
Eonje kkeunnalkkayo?

'커트'는 '컷'이라고도 부르고, '파마'는 '펌'이라고 부르기도 해요. 보통 머리를 곧게 펴는 것(straightening hair)을 '매직 스트레이트 펌'이나 '매직'이라고 해요.

11

Making friends 친구 사귀기

Becoming friends with people you meet while traveling
can also become a precious memory.
Let's try greeting them first.

Hello. Nice to meet you.

안녕하세요. 만나서 반갑습니다.
Annyeonghaseyo. Mannaseo bangapseumnida.

I am a student/an office worker.

저는 학생/회사원입니다.
Jeoneun haksaeng/hoesawonimnida.

I came to Korea for travel.

한국에 여행하러 왔어요.
Hanguge yeohaenghareo wasseoyo.

I will be traveling in Korea until next month.

다음 달까지 한국을 여행할 거예요.
Da-eum dalkkaji hangugeul yeohaenghal geoyeyo.

I came with friends/with family/alone.

친구와/가족들과/혼자 왔어요.
Chinguwa/gajokdeulgwa/honja wasseoyo.

I have been/have never been to Korea before.

전에 한국에 온 적 있어요/없어요.
Jeone hanguge on jeok isseoyo/eopseoyo.

This is my friend.

이쪽은 제 친구예요.
Ijjogeun je chinguyeyo.

I don't speak Korean well.

한국어는 잘 못해요.

Hangugeoneun jal motaeyo.

I look forward to getting to know you.

잘 부탁합니다.

Jal butakamnida.

Useful Words

초등학생 chodeunghaksaeng elementary school student	**중학생** junghaksaeng middle school student	**고등학생** godeunghaksaeng high school student
대학생 daehaksaeng university student	**주부** jubu housewife	**회사원** hoesawon office worker
교사 gyosa teacher	**은행원** eunhaengwon bank teller	**의사** uisa doctor
변호사 byeonhosa lawyer	**디자이너** dijaineo designer	**자영업자** jayeong-eopja self-employed
공무원 gongmuwon public servant	**요리사** yorisa chef	**미용사** miyongsa hairdresser
모델 model model	**군인** gunin soldier	**기자** gija journalist

🎧 MP3 11-2

Let me introduce my family.

제 가족을 소개할게요.

Je gajogeul sogaehalgeyo.

This is my child/husband/wife.

제 아이예요/남편이에요/아내예요.

Je aiyeyo/nampyeonieyo/anaeyeyo.

These are my parents.

저희 부모님이세요.

Jeohi bumonimiseyo.

> **Tip**
> '우리'를 높여서 말할 때(in polite speech), '저희'를 사용해요.

Our family has four members in total.

우리 가족은 모두 네 명입니다.

Uri gajogeun modu ne myeong-imnida.

This person is my older brother.

이 사람은 제 오빠/형입니다.

I sarameun je oppa/hyeong-imnida.

This person is my older sister.

이 사람은 제 누나/언니입니다.

I sarameun je nuna/eonniimnida.

This person is my younger brother.

이 사람은 제 남동생입니다.

I sarameun je namdongsaeng-imnida.

This person is my younger sister.

이 사람은 제 여동생입니다.
I sarameun je yeodongsaeng-imnida.

I don't have any siblings.

저는 형제자매가 없어요.
Jeoneun hyeongjejamaega eopseoyo.

Your daughter/son is very cute.

따님/아드님이 아주 귀엽네요.
Ttanim/adeunim-i aju gwiyeomneyo.

Tip

다른 사람의 딸이나 아들을 높여서 말할 때 '따님'이나 '아드님'이라는 말을 사용해요.

엄마 / 어머니
eomma / eomeoni
mom / mother

남동생
namdongsaeng
younger brother

할머니
halmeoni
grandmother

아빠 / 아버지
appa / abeoji
dad / father

할아버지
harabeoji
grandfather

나
na
I, myself

What is your name?

성함이 어떻게 되세요?
Seonghami eotteoke doeseyo?

Where do you live?

댁은 어디세요?
Daegeun eodiseyo?

Tip

'성함'은 '이름'을 높여서 부르는 말(in polite speech)이고, '댁'은 '집'을 높여서 부르는 말이에요.

Is your school/workplace nearby?

학교는/직장은 이 근처에 있어요?
Hakgyoneun/jikjang-eun i geuncheoe isseoyo?

May I ask how old you are?

몇 살인지 물어봐도 될까요?
Myeot sarinji mureobwado doelkkayo?

We're the same age.

저랑 동갑이네요.
Jeorang donggabineyo.

Are you a student/employed?

학생/직장인이세요?
Haksaeng/jikjang-iniseyo?

If you don't mind me asking, are you married?

실례지만, 결혼하셨어요?
Sillyejiman, gyeolhonhasyeosseoyo?

Could I get your contact information?

연락처를 알 수 있을까요?
Yeollakcheoreul al su isseulkkayo?

Can I have your KakaoTalk/Instagram ID?

카톡/인스타 ID를 알 수 있을까요?
Katok/inseuta IDreul al su isseulkkayo?

Where is your hometown?

고향은 어디예요?
Gohyang-eun eodiyeyo?

Tip

'카톡'은 한국에서 가장 많이 사용하는 메시저 어플(messaging app)인 카카오톡(Kakao Talk)을 줄여서 부르는 말이에요. '인스타'는 '인스타그램(Instagram)'을 줄여서 부르는 말이에요.

What do you do for a living?

어떤 일을 하세요?
Eotteon ireul haseyo?

Do you like coffee?

커피를 좋아하세요?
Keopireul joahaseyo?

What kind of music do you like?

이떤 음악을 좋아하세요?
Eotteon eumageul joahaseyo?

What's your MBTI?

MBTI가 뭐예요?
MBTIga mwoyeyo?

Do you happen to have time tomorrow?

혹시 내일 시간 있어요?

Hoksi naeil sigan isseoyo?

Would you like to have coffee together?

같이 커피 한잔 할래요?

Gachi keopi hanjan hallaeyo?

How about going to see a movie together?

같이 영화 보러 가면 어때요?

Gachi yeonghwa boreo gamyeon eottaeyo?

Could you go shopping with me?

쇼핑하러 같이 가 줄 수 있어요?

Syopinghareo gachi ga jul su isseoyo?

What time works for you?

몇 시에 시간 괜찮아요?

Myeot sie sigan gwaenchanayo?

Let's meet at the cafe at 3 PM.

오후 3시에 카페에서 만나요.

Ohu se sie kapeeseo mannayo.

It's the cafe next to the bakery over there.

저기 빵집 옆에 있는 카페요.

Jeogi ppangjip yeope inneun kapeyo.

I just created an Instagram account.

이번에 인스타 계정을 만들었어요.

Ibeone inseuta gyejeong-eul mandeureosseoyo.

Please follow my account.

제 계정을 팔로우해 주세요.

Je gyejeong-eul pallouhae juseyo.

I've just uploaded a photo. Did you see it?

방금 사진을 하나 올렸어요. 봤어요?

Banggeum sajineul hana ollyeosseoyo. Bwasseoyo?

I'll leave lots of comments for you too.

댓글도 자주 달아 줄게요.

Daetgeuldo jaju dara julgeyo.

Did you check the DM I sent?

DM 보낸 거 확인했어요?

DM bonaen geo hwaginhaesseoyo?

Tip

'프사'는 SNS 계정(accounts)에서 자신의 개성(individuality)을 나타낼 수 있는 사진인 '프로필 사진(profile picture)'이 줄임말이에요.

I changed my profile picture to a photo taken with a friend.

친구랑 찍은 사진으로 프사를 바꿨어요.

Chingurang jjigeun sajineuro peusareul bakkwosseoyo.

I hope my number of followers increases.

팔로우 수가 더 늘어나면 좋겠어요.

Pallou suga deo neureonamyeon jokesseoyo.

MP3 11-6

What are your plans for the weekend?

주말 계획이 어떻게 되세요?

Jumal gyehoegi eotteoke doeseyo?

What do you usually do on weekends?

주말에 보통 무엇을 해요?

Jumare botong mueoseul haeyo?

What are you going to do this weekend?

이번 주말에 뭐 할 거예요?

Ibeon jumare mwo hal geoyeyo?

I'm going to rest at home.

집에서 쉴 거예요.

Jibeseo swil geoyeyo.

I plan to meet my family.

가족을 만나려고요.

Gajogeul mannaryeogoyo.

I'm thinking of going hiking.

등산을 갈까 해요.

Deungsaneul galkka haeyo.

I'm going to visit a friend's house.

친구 집에 놀러갈 거예요.

Chingu jibe nolleogal geoyeyo.

I don't have any special plans yet.

아직 특별한 계획은 없어요.
Ajik teukbyeolhan gyehoegeun eopseoyo.

I'm thinking of doing some exercise.

운동을 좀 할 생각이에요.
Undong-eul jom hal saenggagieyo.

Useful Words		

독서를 하다	dokseoreul hada	to read
등산을 하다	deungsaneul hada	to go hiking
미술관에 가다	misulgwane gada	to go to an art gallery
밀린 일을 하다	millin ireul hada	to catch up on work
박물관에 가다	bangmulgwane gada	to go to a museum
산책을 하다	sanchaegeul hada	to take a walk
여행을 가다	yeohaeng-eul gada	to go traveling
영화를 보다	yeonghwareul boda	to watch a movie
전시회를 보다	jeonsihoereul boda	to see an exhibition
콘서트를 보다	konseoteureul boda	to attend a concert

Have you ever tried making Korean food?

한국 음식을 만들어 본 적 있어요?

Hanguk eumsigeul mandeureo bon jeok isseoyo?

Have you ever lived in a foreign country?

외국에서 살아 본 적 있어요?

Oegugeseo sara bon jeok isseoyo?

Have you ever learned a foreign language?

외국어를 배운 적 있어요?

Oegugeoreul baeun jeok isseoyo?

Have you ever made friends while traveling?

여행 중에 친구를 사귄 적 있어요?

Yeohaeng jung-e chingureul sagwin jeok isseoyo?

How was your first time traveling abroad?

처음 해외 여행을 했을 때 어땠어요?

Cheoeum haeoe yeohaeng-eul haesseul ttae eottaesseoyo?

Which country did you like best among those you've visited?

가 봤던 나라 중에 어디가 제일 좋았어요?

Ga bwatdeon nara jung-e eodiga jeil joasseoyo?

What's the most delicious food you've ever tasted?

먹어 본 음식 중에 가장 맛있었던 게 뭐예요?

Meogeo bon eumsik jung-e gajang masisseotdeon ge mwoyeyo?

Have you ever learned to play a musical instrument?

악기를 배워 본 적 있어요?
Akgireul baewo bon jeok isseoyo?

Have you ever been to a concert?

콘서트에 가 본 적 있어요?
Konseoteu-e ga bon jeok isseoyo?

Have you ever gone camping?

캠핑을 해 본 적 있어요?
Kaemping-eul hae bon jeok isseoyo?

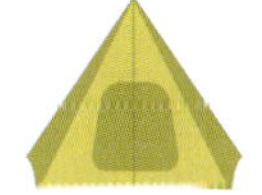

Have you ever met a famous person?

유명한 사람을 만나 본 적 있어요?
Yumyeonghan sarameul manna bon jeok isseoyo?

Have you ever tried bungee jumping?

번지 점프를 해 본 적 있어요?
Beonji jeompeureul hae bon jeok isseoyo?

Have you ever watched a sports game at a stadium?

경기장에서 스포츠 경기를 본 적 있어요?
Gyeonggijang-eseo seupocheu gyeonggireul bon jeok isseoyo?

Have you ever learned to dance before?

예전에 춤을 배워 본 적 있어요?
Yejeone chumeul baewo bon jeok isseoyo?

■ **What's your ideal type?**

이상형이 어떻게 되세요?
Isanghyeong-i eotteoke doeseyo?

My ideal type is a caring person.

제 이상형은 자상한 사람이에요.
Je isanghyeong-eun jasanghan saramieyo.

I like someone who makes me laugh often.

저를 자주 웃게 만드는 사람이 좋아요.
Jeoreul jaju utge mandeuneun sarami joayo.

People with a short temper are not my style.

성격이 급한 사람은 제 스타일이 아니에요.
Seonggyeogi geupan sarameun je seutairi anieyo.

I'm attracted to cute people.

저는 귀여운 사람한테 끌려요.
Jeoneun gwiyeoun saramhante kkeullyeoyo.

I'm looking for someone who's faithful and honest.

저는 성실하고 정직한 사람을 찾고 있어요.
Jeoneun seongsilhago jeongjikan sarameul chatgo isseoyo.

I consider good communication to be important.

저는 대화가 잘 통하는 것을 중요하게 생각해요.
Jeoneun daehwaga jal tonghaneun geoseul jungyohage saenggakhaeyo.

Useful Words

저는 [ ] 사람이 좋아요.

I like people who are (   )

독립적인	dongnipjeogin	independent
똑똑한	ttokttokan	smart
마음이 넓은	ma-eumi neolbeun	open-minded
배려심 있는	baeryeosim inneun	caring
성실한	seongsilhan	faithful / sincere
자신감 있는	jasingam inneun	confident
재미있는	jaemiinneun	funny
정직한	jeongjikhan	honest
친절한	chinjeolhan	kind

[ ] 사람은 제 스타일이 아니에요.

People who are (   ) aren't my style.

거만한	geomanhan	arrogant
거짓말하는	geojinmalhaneun	dishonest
게으른	ge-eureun	lazy
고집 센	gojip sen	stubborn
부정적인	bujeongjeogin	negative
소심한	sosimhan	timid
이기적인	igijeogin	selfish
잔인한	janinhan	cruel
질투심 많은	jillusim maneun	jealous

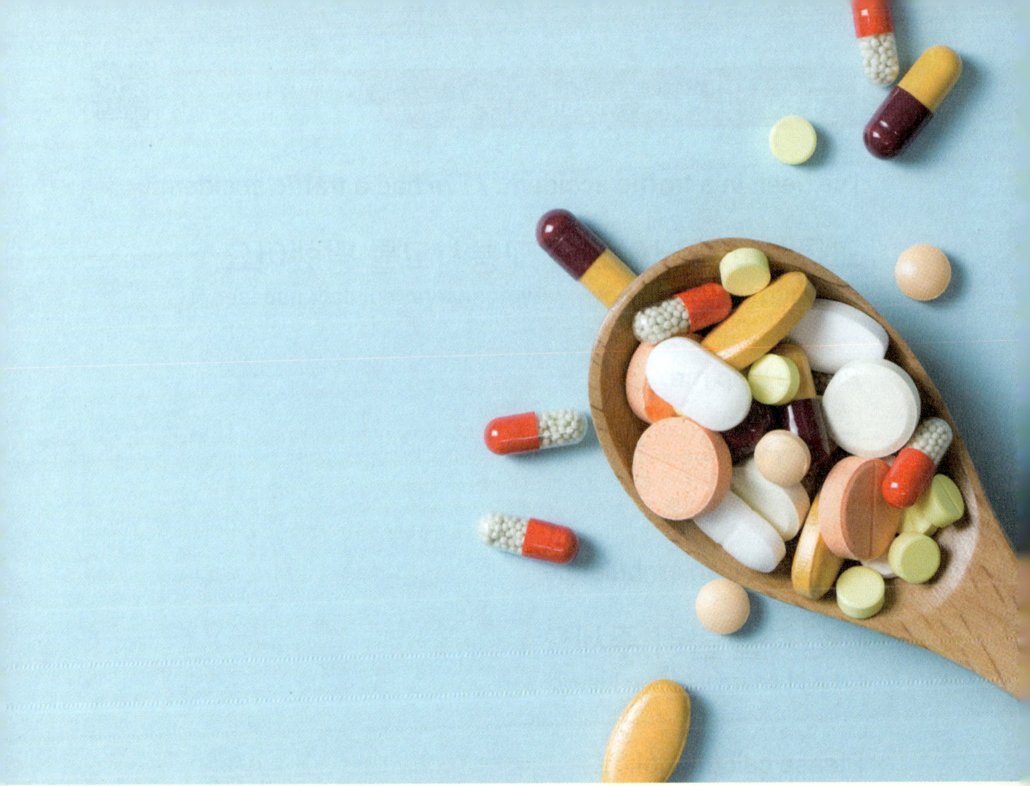

12

Emergency 비상 상황

It's best if no emergency situations arise while abroad,
but it's still good to prepare thoroughly
just in case of any unexpected events.

🎧 MP3 12-1

I've been in a traffic accident. / I've had a traffic accident.

교통사고가 났어요. / 교통사고를 당했어요.

Gyotongsagoga nasseoyo. / Gyotongsagoreul danghaesseoyo.

Please help me.

도와주세요.

Dowajuseyo.

Please call an ambulance.

구급차를 불러 주세요.

Gugeupchareul bulleo juseyo.

Please call the police.

경찰을 불러 주세요.

Gyeongchareul bulleo juseyo.

I have/don't have travel insurance.

여행자 보험이 있어요/없어요.

Yeohaengja boheomi isseoyo/eopseoyo.

Please take me to the hospital.

병원으로 데려다주세요.

Byeongwoneuro deryeoda juseyo.

My emergency contact information is here.

비상 연락처는 여기에 있어요.

Bisang yeollakcheoneun yeogie isseoyo.

☆ Terms related to car accidents

가해자	gahaeja	perpetrator
견인차	gyeonincha	tow truck
목격자	mokgyeokja	witness
부딪히다	budichida	to collide
부상	busang	injury
블랙박스	beullaekbakseu	black box
속도 위반	sokdo wiban	speeding
안전벨트	anjeon belteu	seatbelt
접촉 사고	jeopchok sago	fender bender
음주 운전	eumju unjeon	drunk driving
피해자	pihaeja	victim
합의	habui	settlement

교통사고가 발생한다면 아무리 작은 사고라도 반드시 경찰과 보험사 (insurance company)에 연락하고, 병원을 방문해서 기록(record)을 남겨 두어야 해요. 한국어를 잘 못해서 도움이 필요하면 사고 현장(the scene of the accident)에서 통역 서비스(interpretation services)를 요청하거나 외국인종합안내센터(Korea Immigration Contact Center, 1345)에 연락해서 전화 상담 서비스를 받을 수 있어요.

🎧 **MP3** 12-2

■ **Where does it hurt? / Where are you feeling discomfort?**

어디가 아프세요/불편하세요?
Eodiga apeuseyo/bulpyeonhaseyo?

I feel like I'm coming down with a cold.

감기 기운이 있어요.
Gamgi giuni isseoyo.

I have a fever.

열이 나요.
Yeori nayo.

I'm coughing.

기침을 해요.
Gichimeul haeyo.

My throat hurts.

목이 아파요.
Mogi apayo.

I've twisted my ankle.

발목을 삐었어요.
Balmogeul ppieosseoyo.

I've injured my arm.

팔을 다쳤어요.
Pareul dachyeosseoyo.

My stomach hurts.

배가 아파요.
Baega apayo.

I have severe constipation/diarrhea.

변비/설사가 심해요.
Byeonbi/seolsa-ga simhaeyo.

This part/my whole body is itchy.

여기가/온몸이 가려워요.
Yeogiga/onmomi garyeowoyo.

I've been burned by something hot.

뜨거운 것에 데였어요.
Tteugeoun geose deyeosseoyo.

I'm having an allergic reaction.

알레르기 반응이 있어요.
Allereugi baneung-i isseoyo.

I'm having difficulty breathing.

숨 쉬기가 힘들어요.
Sum swigiga himdeureoyo.

I feel like I'm going to vomit.

토할 것 같아요.
Tohal geot gatayo.

3. 병원 치료 Medical treatment

🎧 MP3 12-3

■ **When did your symptoms start?**

언제부터 증상이 있었나요?
Eonjebuteo jeungsang-i isseonnayo?

■ **Do you have any other symptoms?**

혹시 다른 증상은 없어요?
Hoksi dareun jeungsang-eun eopseoyo?

■ **I'll take your temperature.**

열을 재 볼게요.
Yeoreul jae bolgeyo.

■ **Are you insured?**

보험에 가입되어 있습니까?
Boheome gaipdoe-eo itseumnikka?

■ **You need to be hospitalized.**

입원해야 합니다.
Ibwonhaeya hamnida.

■ **You need surgery.**

수술이 필요합니다.
Susuri piryohamnida.

When can I be discharged?

언제 퇴원할 수 있어요?
Eonje toewonhal su isseoyo?

■ **Do you have any pre-existing medical conditions?**

평소에 앓고 있는 병이 있습니까?
Pyeongsoe alko inneun byeong-i itseumnikka?

I have anemia.

빈혈이 있어요.
Binhyeori isseoyo.

I have low blood pressure/high blood pressure.

저혈압/고혈압이에요.
Jeohyeorap/gohyeorabieyo.

■ **Do you take any medications regularly?**

평소에 먹는 약이 있습니까?
Pyeongsoe meongneun yagi itseumnikka?

I take dermatology medication.

피부과 약을 먹고 있어요.
Pibugwa yageul meokgo isseoyo.

■ **Here's your prescription.**

처방진 어기 있습니다.
Cheobangjeon yeogi itseumnida.

■ **Take this medication and come back in 3 days.**

약을 드시고 3일 후에 다시 오세요.
Yageul deusigo sam il hue dasi oseyo.

내과	naegwa	internal medicine
산부인과	sanbuingwa	obstetrics and gynecology
소아과	soagwa	pediatrics
신경과	singyeonggwa	neurology
안과	angwa	ophthalmology
외과	oegwa	surgery
응급의학과	eunggeubeuihakgwa	emergency medicine
이비인후과	ibiinhugwa	otolaryngology
정신과	jeongsingwa	psychiatry
정형외과	jeonghyeong-oegwa	orthopedics
치과	chigwa	dentistry
피부과	pibugwa	dermatology

검사하다	geomsahada	to examine / to run tests
수술하다	susulhada	to undergo surgery / to operate
약을 처방받다	yageul cheobangbatda	to get a prescription
응급실에 가다	eunggeupsire gada	to go to the emergency room
입원하다	ibwonhada	to be hospitalized
주사를 맞다	jusareul matda	to get an injection
진찰을 받다	jinchareul batda	to get a medical examination
치료를 받다	chiryoreul batda	to receive treatment
퇴원하다	toewonhada	to be discharged from the hospital

4. 분실 · 신고 Lost and found

I've lost my wallet.

지갑을 잃어버렸어요.
Jigabeul ireobeoryeosseoyo.

My phone is missing.

휴대폰이 없어졌어요.
Hyudaeponi eopseojyeosseoyo.

My wallet was stolen.

지갑을 도둑맞았어요.
Jigabeul doduk majasseoyo.

Where did you lose it?

어디에서 잃어버렸어요?
Eodieseo ireobeoryeosseoyo?

I think I lost it at the department store/restaurant.

백화점/식당에서 잃어버린 것 같아요.
Baekwajeom/Sikdang-eseo ireobeorin geot gatayo.

I'm not sure.

잘 모르겠어요.
Jal moreugesseoyo.

I think I left it on the subway.

지하철에 두고 내린 것 같아요.
Jihacheore dugo naerin geot gatayo.

Where do I report lost items?

분실물 신고는 어디에 해야 하나요?
Bunsilmul singoneun eodie haeya hanayo?

I lost my bag. Is it possible to find it?

가방을 잃어버렸는데 찾을 수 있을까요?
Gabang-eul ireobeoryeonneunde chajeul su isseulkkayo?

Oh, this is it. Thank you.

아, 이거예요. 감사합니다.
A, igeoyeyo. Gamsahamnida.

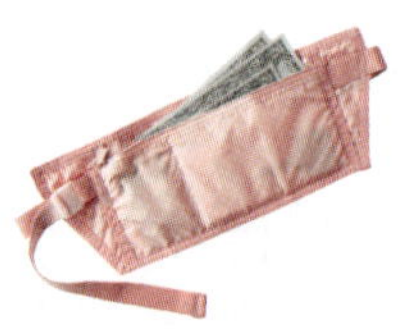

Tip **지하철에서 물건을 잃어버렸을 때** When You Lose an Item on the Subway

지하철을 이용하면서 물건을 잃어버렸거나 누군가가 잃어버린 물건을 주운 경우에 유실물센터(Lost and Found Center)를 이용하거나 경찰청 유실물 종합 안내(Police Lost and Found Comprehensive Guide)를 이용하면 돼요. 유실물센터는 1, 2호선 시청역(City Hall Station), 3, 4호선 충무로역(Chungmuro Station), 5, 8호선 왕십리역(Wangsimni Station), 6, 7호선 태릉입구역(Taereung Station)에 있어요. 운영 시간은 평일(weekdays) 오전 9시에서 오후 6시까지예요.

5. 아이가 없어졌다 Lost child

My child is missing.

아이가 없어졌어요.
Aiga eopseojyeosseoyo.

Please make an announcement to find her.

아이를 찾는 방송을 해 주세요.
Aireul channeun bangsong-eul hae juseyo.

She's a 5-year-old girl.

5살 여자아이예요.
Daseot sal yeojaaiyeyo.

Here's a photo of the child.

아이의 사진은 여기에 있어요.
Aiui sajineun yeogie isseoyo.

She's wearing a red T-shirt and blue pants.

빨간색 티셔츠와 파란색 바지를 입고 있어요.
Ppalgansaek tisyeocheuwa paransaek bajireul ipgo isseoyo.

She's carrying a yellow backpack.

노란색 가방을 메고 있어요.
Noransaek gabang-eul mego isseoyo.

She went missing on the 2nd floor of the department store.

백화점 2층에서 없어졌어요.
Baekwajeom i cheung-eseo eopseojyeosseoyo.

6. 여권을 잃어버렸다 Lost passport

🎧 MP3 12-6

I've lost my passport.

여권을 잃어버렸어요.
Yeogwoneul ireobeoryeosseoyo.

I need to go to the nearest police station to report the loss.

가까운 경찰서에 가서 분실 신고를 해야 해요.
Gakkaun gyeongchalseo-e gaseo bunsil singoreul haeya haeyo.

I want to contact the embassy. What's their number?

대사관에 연락하려는데 번호가 어떻게 되죠?
Daesagwane yeollakaryeoneunde beonhoga eotteoke doejyo?

■ **You need a photo to issue a temporary passport.**

여권을 발급하려면 사진이 필요해요.
Yeogwoneul balgeuparyeomyeon sajini piryohaeyo.

I don't have a photo. Is there a photo studio nearby?

사진이 없는데, 근처에 사진관 있어요?
Sajini eomneunde, geuncheo-e sajingwan isseoyo?

Please re-issue my passport.

여권을 재발급해 주세요.
Yeogwoneul jaebalgeupae juseyo.

How long does it take to re-issue a passport?

재발급에 시간이 얼마나 걸려요?
Jaebalgeube sigani eolmana geollyeoyo?

(When asking a stranger for directions) **I'm lost.**

(행인에게 길을 물을 때) 길을 잃어버렸어요.
Gireul ireobeoryeosseoyo.

Where am I?

여기가 어디인가요?
Yeogiga eodiingayo?

How do I get to the nearest subway station?

가까운 지하철역까지 어떻게 가요?
Gakkaun jihacheoryeokkkaji eotteoke gayo?

I can't understand the map well.

지도를 봐도 잘 모르겠어요.
Jidoreul bwado jal moreugesseoyo.

Could you please look at this map?

이 지도를 좀 봐 주세요.
I jidoreul jom bwa juseyo.

Could you accompany me to somewhere nearby?

근처까지 같이 가 줄 수 있을까요?
Geuncheokkaji gachi ga jul su isseulkkayo?

I'm sorry, but could you call a taxi for me?

죄송한데 택시를 불러 줄 수 있어요?
Joesonghande taeksireul bulleo jul su isseoyo?

(When asking a friend for directions) **I can see a post office nearby.**

(친구에게 길을 물을 때) 근처에 우체국이 보여요.
Geuncheo-e uchegugi boyeoyo.

This is 5 Haengbok-ro 1-gil.

여기 행복로 1길 5번지예요.
Yeogi haengbongno il gil o beonjiyeyo.

How do I get there from here?

여기에서 어떻게 가면 돼요?
Yeogieseo eotteoke gamyeon dwaeyo?

Should I turn left at the main street?

큰길에서 왼쪽으로 가면 될까요?
Keungireseo oenjjogeuro gamyeon doelkkayo?

I'm not sure about the direction.

방향을 잘 모르겠어요.
Banghyang-eul jal moreugesseoyo.

I'll ask someone passing by.

지나가는 사람한테 물어볼게요.
Jinaganeun saramhante mureobolgeyo.

Oh, I understand now.

아, 이제 알겠어요.
A, ije algesseoyo.

Help me.

도와주세요.
Dowajuseyo.

Come quickly.

빨리 와 주세요.
Ppalli wa juseyo.

It's urgent. Please hurry.

급해요. 서둘러 주세요.
Geupaeyo. Seodulleo juseyo.

Please call the police.

경찰을 불러 주세요.
Gyeongchareul bulleo juseyo.

Please call someone who can help.

도와줄 사람을 불러 주세요.
Dowajul sarameul bulleo juseyo.

Fire! There's a fire.

불이야! 불이 났어요.
Buriya! Buri nasseoyo.

It's an earthquake.

지진입니다.
Jijinimnida.

Someone is injured.

사람이 다쳤어요.
Sarami dachyeosseoyo.

Someone has collapsed.

사람이 쓰러졌어요.
Sarami sseureojyeosseoyo.

Someone has fallen into the water.

사람이 물에 빠졌어요.
Sarami mure ppajyeosseoyo.

A strange person is following me.

이상한 사람이 따라와요.
Isanghan sarami ttarawayo.

I was hit by a stranger.

모르는 사람한테 맞았어요.
Moreuneun saramhante majasseoyo.

I think someone entered my room.

방에 누가 들어왔던 것 같아요.
Bang-e nuga deureowatdeon geot gatayo.

The door won't open. I'm trapped in here.

문이 안 열려요. 여기에 갇혔어요.
Muni an yeollyeoyo. Yeogie gachyeosseoyo.

9. 경찰서에서 At the police station

I'm here to file a report.

신고하러 왔어요.
Singohareo wasseoyo.

I've been scammed/defrauded.

사기를 당했어요.
Sagireul danghaesseoyo.

That person is the culprit.

저 사람이 범인이에요.
Jeo sarami beominieyo.

I saw it myself.

제가 직접 봤어요.
Jega jikjeop bwasseoyo.

It happened this afternoon.

오늘 오후에 있었던 일이에요.
Oneul ohue isseotdeon irieyo.

Here is my name and contact information.

제 이름과 연락처 여기 있습니다.
Je ireumgwa yeollakcheo yeogi itseumnida.

Please contact me if you need any additional information.

수가 정보가 필요하면 연락 주세요.
Chuga jeongboga piryohamyeon yeollak juseyo.

Are you okay?

괜찮으세요?

Gwaenchaneuseyo?

You must have been through a lot.

많이 힘드셨죠?

Mani himdeusyeotjyo?

Calm down.

진정하세요.

Jinjeonghaseyo.

Don't worry.

걱정 마세요.

Geokjeong maseyo.

It's all right. / Rest assured.

안심하세요.

Ansimhaseyo.

I've reported it to the police.

경찰에 신고했어요.

Gyeongchare singohaesseoyo.

Is there anything I can do to help?

제가 도와 드릴 일 있을까요?

Jegadowa deuril il isseulkkayo?

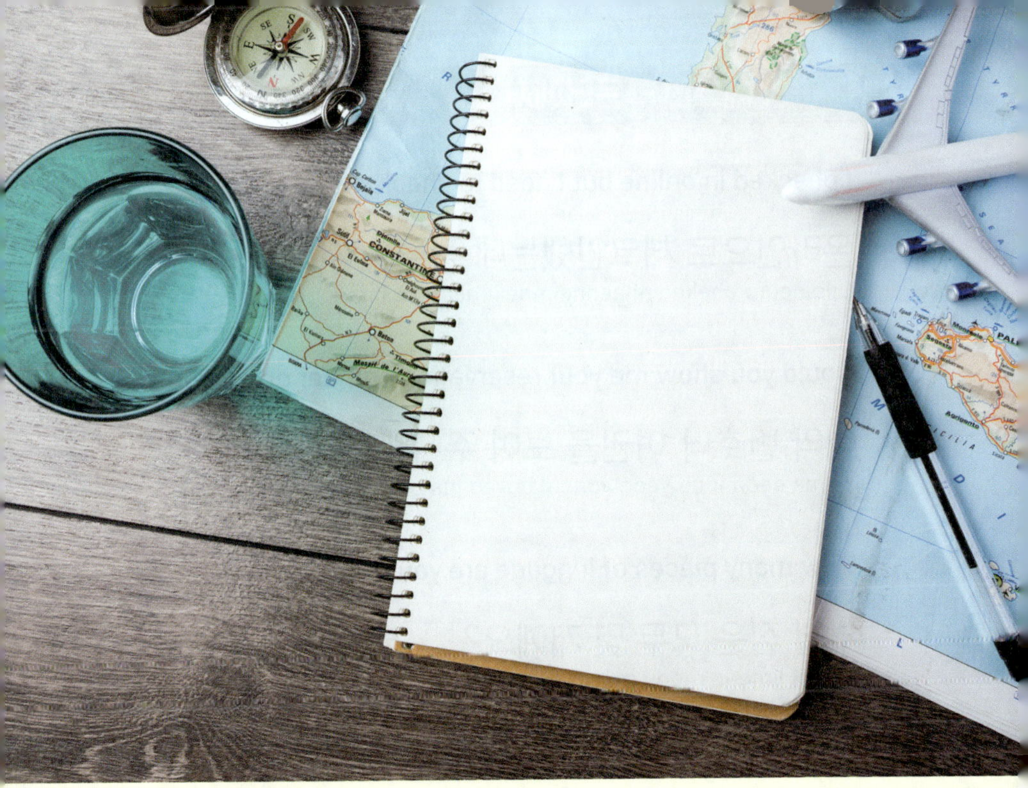

13

Returning 귀국

Time to return to your daily life after an enjoyable journey.
Savor the joy of your smooth travels until the very end.

🎧 MP3 13-1

I checked in online but I need to check my luggage.

온라인으로 체크인했는데 짐을 부치려고요.

Ollaineuro chekeuinhaenneunde jimeul buchiryeogoyo.

Could you show me your reservation number or passport?

예약 번호나 여권을 보여 주시겠어요?

Yeyak beonhona yeogwoneul boyeo jusigesseoyo?

How many pieces of luggage are you checking in?

부칠 짐은 모두 몇 개예요?

Buchil jimeun modu myeot gaeyeyo?

Just this one bag.

이 가방 하나예요.

I gabang hanayeyo.

Please place your luggage on the scale.

짐을 저울 위에 올려 주세요.

Jimeul jeoul wie ollyeo juseyo.

It's 5 kg overweight, so there will be an additional fee.

5kg 초과해서 추가 요금이 있습니다.

O killogeuraem chogwahaeseo chuga yogeumi itseumnida.

There are no cigarettes or batteries in your luggage, right?

수화물에 담배나 배터리 등은 없으시죠?

Suhwamure dambaena baeteori deung-eun eopseusijyo?

■ **Your boarding gate is B12.**

탑승 게이트는 B12입니다.
Tapseung geiteuneun Biriimnida.

■ **Boarding closes one hour before departure.**

탑승은 출발 1시간 전에 마감됩니다.
Tapseung-eun chulbal han sigan jeone magamdoemnida.

Where is the airport duty-free shop?

공항 면세점은 어디에 있어요?
Gonghang myeonsejeomeun eodie isseoyo?

■ **It's straight ahead after you pass through security.**

보안 검사를 통과하신 후에 직진하시면 바로 있습니다.
Boan geomsareul tonggwahasin hue jikjinhasimyeon baro itseumnida.

Tip **온라인 체크인** Online Check-in Services

대부분의 항공사(airlines)는 출발 24시간 전부터 온라인 체크인 서비스를 제공하고 있어요. 공항에서 길게 줄을 서서 기다릴 필요 없이 간단하게 온라인으로 체크인을 진행하고 모바일 탑승권(mobile boarding pass)을 받을 수 있다는 장점(advantage)이 있어요. 공항에 있는 키오스크(kiosks)를 통해 셀프 체크인(self check-in)하는 것도 가능해요. 이용 제한 승객(restricted passenger)이 아니면 자동 수하물 위탁 기기(automated baggage drop-off machines)를 이용해 직접 짐을 부치는 것도 가능해요.

🎧 MP3 13-2

Is this Lotte Duty Free?

여기 롯데면세점이에요?
Yeogi rotdemyeonsejeomieyo?

No, Lotte Duty Free is to the left.

아니요, 롯데면세점은 왼쪽으로 가세요.
Aniyo, rotdemyeonsejeomeun oenjjogeuro gaseyo.

I purchased through the app. Do I pick up my items here?

어플로 구입했는데 물건은 여기서 찾아요?
Eopeullo guipaenneunde mulgeoneun yeogiseo chajayo?

No, this is where you buy items.

아니요, 여기는 물건을 구입하는 매장이에요.
Aniyo, yeogineun mulgeoneul guipaneun maejang-ieyo.

To pick up your products, please go up to the second floor.

상품을 찾으시려면 2층으로 올라가세요.
Sangpumeul chajeusiryeomyeon i cheung-euro ollagaseyo.

Please take a number and wait.

번호표를 먼저 뽑고 기다려 주세요.
Beonhopyoreul meonjeo ppopgo gidaryeo juseyo.

Can I see your passport and boarding pass?

여권이랑 탑승권을 보여 주세요.
Yeogwonirang tapseunggwoneul boyeo juseyo.

I want to buy 4 bottles of alcohol. Will I have trouble at customs?

술을 4병 사려는데 세관에 걸릴까요?
Sureul ne byeong saryeoneunde segwane geollilkkayo?

Only 2 bottles of alcohol per person are duty-free.

술은 1인당 2병까지만 면세입니다.
Sureun il indang du byeongkkajiman myeonseimnida.

Is this all the types of face masks you have?

마스크팩 종류는 여기 있는 게 다예요?
Maseukeupaek jongnyuneun yeogi inneun ge dayeyo?

Yes, all available products are on display.

네, 전시된 제품이 전부입니다.
Ne, jeonsidoen jepumi jeonbuimnida.

How would you like to pay?

계산은 어떻게 하시겠습니까?
Gyesaneun eotteoke hasigetseumnikka?

I'll pay in dollars/Korean won.

달러로/원으로 지불할게요.
Dalleoro/woneuro jibulhalgeyo.

Please don't open the packaging until you arrive at your destination.

포장은 도착하시면 뜯어 주세요.
Pojang-eun dochakasimyeon tteudeo juseyo.

온라인 면세점에서 물건을 구입하면 편리할 뿐 아니라 다양한 할인 쿠폰 (discount coupons)을 받을 수 있는 장점이 있어요. 단, 구입한 상품은 출발 게이트(departure gate)에서만 받을 수 있다는 점을 기억하세요. 출발 전까지만 받을 수 있으므로, 미리 면세점 인도장(pickup counter)의 위치를 확인하고 비행기를 타기 전에 여유있게 시간을 계획해 두는 게 좋아요.

상품 수령 안내 (Product Pickup Guide)

Step 1   면세점 인도장(pickup counter)에 방문하세요.

Step 2   교환권(voucher)과 자신의 여권을 보여 주세요.

Step 3   여권과 출국 정보(departure information)가 맞는지 확인 받으세요.

Step 4   상품을 받고 서명하세요.(sign)

Step 5   상품 수령이 끝났어요.

Appendix 부록

Vocabulary by category

1월	irwol	January
2월	iwol	February
3월	samwol	March
4월	sawol	April
5월	owol	May
6월	yuwol	June
7월	chirwol	July
8월	parwol	August
9월	guwol	September
10월	siwol	October
11월	sibirwol	November
12월	sibiwol	December
월요일	woryoil	Monday
화요일	hwayoil	Tuesday
수요일	suyoil	Wednesday
목요일	mogyoil	Thursday
금요일	geumyoil	Friday
토요일	toyoil	Saturday
일요일	iryoil	Sunday
봄	bom	spring
여름	yeoreum	summer
가을	ga-eul	fall
겨울	gyeoul	winter
그저께	geujeokke	the day before yesterday

내일	naeil	tomorrow
다음주	da-eumju	next week
대략	daeryak	approximately
때때로	ttaettaero	sometimes
매달	maedal	every month
매일	maeil	every day
매주	maeju	every week
모레	more	the day after tomorrow
무슨 요일	museun yoil	which day
밤	bam	night
어제	eoje	yesterday
언제나	eonjena	always
오늘	oneul	today
오전	ojeon	morning (AM)
오후	ohu	afternoon (PM)
이번 주	ibeon ju	this week
일주일	iljuil	one week
저녁	jeonyeok	evening
종종	jongjong	often
주말	jumal	weekend
지금	jigeum	now
지난주	jinanju	last week
평일	pyeong-il	weekday, business day
하루 종일	haru jong-il	all day
깊은 밤	gipeun bam	deep at night

남쪽	namjjok	south
대각선	daegakseon	diagonal line
대각선 오른쪽	daegakseon oreunjjok	right on the diagonal line
대각선 왼쪽	daegakseon oenjjok	left on the diagonal line
동서남북	dongseonambuk	all four directions
동쪽	dongjjok	east
뒤쪽	dwijjok	behind
맞은편	majeunpyeon	across
반대 방향	bandae banghyang	opposite direction
반대편	bandaepyeon	opposite side
방향	banghyang	direction
부근(근처)	bugeun (geuncheo)	vicinity
북쪽	bukjjok	north
상하	sangha	up and down
서쪽	seojjok	west
시계 방향	sigye banghyang	clockwise
시계 반대 방향	sigye bandae banghyang	counterclockwise
아래쪽	araejjok	bottom side
앞쪽	apjjok	front side
옆쪽	yeopjjok	side
오른쪽	oreunjjok	right side
왼쪽	oenjjok	left side
위쪽	wijjok	top side
좌우	jwau	left and right

국가	gukga	nation / country
대만	daeman	Taiwan
대한민국	daehanminguk / hanguk	Korea
도쿄	dokyo	Tokyo
독일	dogil	Germany
말레이시아	malleisia	Malaysia
멕시코	meksiko	Mexico
미국	miguk	America / the U.S.
베이징	beijing	Beijing
벨기에	belgie	Belgium
북한	bukan	North Korea
브라질	beurajil	Brazil
상하이	sanghai	Shanghai
서울	seoul	Seoul
싱가포르	singgaporeu	Singapore
스페인	seupein	Spain
영국	yeongguk	England
이탈리아	itallia	Italy
일본	ilbon	Japan
중국	jungguk	China
캐나다	kaenada	Canada
태국	taeguk	Thailand
프랑스	peurangseu	France
홍콩	hongkong	Hong Kong

Vocabulary

가다	gada	to go
가르치다	gareuchida	to teach
가지다	gajida	to have
갈아타다	garatada	to transfer
걷다	geotda	to walk
걸다	geolda	to hang
걸리다	geollida	to be hung
계시다	gyesida	to be (formal)
고르다	goreuda	to choose
그리다	geurida	to draw
기다리다	gidarida	to wait
끄다	kkeuda	to turn off
끝나다	kkeunnada	to end
나가다	nagada	to go out
(수염이) 나다	(suyeomi) nada	to grow (a beard)
나오다	naoda	to come out
내리다	naerida	to descend
넣다	neota	to put in
놀다	nolda	to play
다녀오다	danyeooda	to go and come back
다니다	danida	to attend
닫다	datda	to close
도와주다	dowajuda	to help
돌아가다	doragada	to go back

돌아오다	doraoda	to come back
돕다	dopda	to help (informal)
되다	doeda	to become
드리다	deurida	to give (formal)
듣다	deutda	to listen
(돈이) 들다	(doni) deulda	to cost
(가방을) 들다	(gabang-eul) deulda	to carry (a bag)
들어가다	deureogada	to enter
들어오다	deureooda	to come in
마시다	masida	to drink
만나다	mannada	to meet
만들다	mandeulda	to make
말다	malda	to stop
맞다	matda	to be correct
먹다	meokda	to eat
모르다	moreuda	to not know
묻다	mutda	to ask
바꾸다	bakkuda	to change
받다	batda	to receive
배우다	baeuda	to learn
보내다	bonaeda	to send
보다	boda	to see
부르다	bureuda	to call
불다	bulda	to blow
빌리다	billida	to borrow

사귀다	sagwida	to make (friends)
사다	sada	to buy
살다	salda	to live
쉬다	swida	to rest
시키다	sikida	to order
신다	sinda	to wear (shoes)
싫어하다	sireohada	to dislike
(글자를) 쓰다	(geuljareul) sseuda	to write (letters)
(컴퓨터를) 쓰다	(keompyuteoreul) sseuda	to use (a computer)
씻다	ssitda	to wash
앉다	anda	to sit
알다	alda	to know
알리다	allida	to inform
열다	yeolda	to open
오다	oda	to come
올라가다	ollagada	to go up
울다	ulda	to cry
웃다	utda	to laugh
일어나다	ireonada	to get up
읽다	ikda	to read
입다	ipda	to wear (clothes)
자다	jada	to sleep
잘하다	jalhada	to do well
잡수시다	japsusida	to eat (formal)
좋아하다	joahada	to like

주다	juda	to give
주무시다	jumusida	to sleep (formal)
지나다	jinada	to pass by
지내다	jinaeda	to spend time
찍다	jjikda	to take (a photo)
찾다	chatda	to find
찾아보다	chajaboda	to search
추다	chuda	to dance
춤추다	chumchuda	to dance
치다	chida	to play (an instrument)
켜다	kyeoda	to turn on
(불에) 타다	(bure) tada	to burn
(차에) 타다	(chae) tada	to ride
팔다	palda	to sell
피우다	piuda	to smoke
하다	hada	to do

가깝다	gakkapda	to be close
가볍다	gabyeopda	to be light
같다	gatda	to be the same
고맙다	gomapda	to be thankful
고프다	gopeuda	to be hungry
괜찮다	gwaenchanta	to be okay
그렇다	geureota	to be so
기쁘다	gippeuda	to be happy
길다	gilda	to be long
깨끗하다	kkaekkeutada	to be clean
나쁘다	nappeuda	to be bad
낮다	natda	to be low
넓다	neolda	to be wide
높다	nopda	to be high
늦다	neutda	to be late
다르다	dareuda	to be different
달다	dalda	to be sweet
덥다	deopda	to be hot
따뜻하다	ttatteutada	to be warm
많다	manta	to be many
맑다	makda	to be clear
맛없다	madeopda	to be not tasty
맛있다	maditda / masitda	to be delicious
맵다	maepda	to be spicy

멀다	meolda	to be far
멋있다	meoditda / meositda	to be cool
무겁다	mugeopda	to be heavy
바쁘다	bappeuda	to be busy
반갑다	bangapda	to be glad
비싸다	bissada	to be expensive
빠르다	ppareuda	to be fast
쉽다	swipda	to be easy
슬프다	seulpeuda	to be sad
시다	sida	to be sour
시원하다	siwonhada	to be refreshing
싫다	silta	to be disliked
싱겁다	singgeopda	to be bland
싸다	ssada	to be cheap
쓰다	sseuda	to be bitter
아니다	anida	to not be
아름답다	areumdapda	to be beautiful
아프다	apeuda	to be sick
어떻다	eotteota	to be how
어렵다	eoryeopda	to be difficult
없다	eopda	to not exist
예쁘다	yeppeuda	to be pretty
작다	jakda	to be small
재미없다	jaemieopda	to be boring
재미있다	jaemiitda	to be interesting

적다	jeokda	to be few
조용하다	joyonghada	to be quiet
좋다	jota	to be good
죄송하다	joesonghada	to be sorry
짜다	jjada	to be salty
춥다	chupda	to be cold
친하다	chinhada	to be close
크다	keuda	to be big
특별하다	teukbyeolhada	to be special
한가하다	hangahada	to be free
흐리다	heurida	to be cloudy

6. 연결하는 말 Connecting words

게다가	gedaga	moreover
그래서	geuraeseo	so
그러나	geureona	however
그러니까	geureonikka	therefore
그러므로	geureomeuro	thus
그러면	geureomyeon	then
그런데	geureonde	but
그렇지만	geureochiman	nevertheless
그리고	geurigo	and
또한	ttohan	also
따라서	ttaraseo	consequently
때문에	ttaemune	because
하지만	hajiman	but

디자인	dijain	design
모자	moja	cap, hat
목도리	mokdori	scarf
무늬	muni	pattern
바지	baji	pants
반바지	banbaji	shorts
반팔	banpal	short-sleeved shirt
블라우스	beullauseu	blouse
셔츠	syeocheu	shirt
스웨터	seuweteo	sweater
양말	yangmal	socks
양복	yangbok	suit
외투	oetu	overcoat
원피스	wonpiseu	dress
장갑	janggap	gloves
점퍼	jeompeo	jacket
정장	jeongjang	formal wear
조끼	jokki	vest
주머니	jumeoni	pocket
청바지	cheongbaji	jeans
치마	chima	skirt
코트	koteu	coat
티셔츠	tisyeocheu	t-shirt
한복	hanbok	hanbok

가습기	gaseupgi	humidifier
건조기	geonjogi	dryer
냉장고	naengjanggo	refrigerator
노트북	noteubuk	laptop
다리미	darimi	iron
디지털 카메라	dijiteol kamera	digital camera
라디오	radio	radio
믹서기	mikseogi	blender
빔 프로젝터	bim peurojekteo	beam projector
선풍기	seonpunggi	fan
세탁기	setakgi	washing machine
스피커	seupikeo	speaker
식기세척기	sikgisecheokgi	dishwasher
신제품	sinjepum	new product
에어컨	e-eokeon	air conditioner
에어프라이어	e-eopeuraieo	air fryer
오븐	obeun	oven
인덕션	indeoksyeon	induction stove
전기밥솥	jeongibapsot	electric rice cooker
전자레인지	jeonjareinji	microwave
청소기	cheongsogi	vacuum cleaner
커피 머신	keopi meosin	coffee machine
텔레비전	tellebijeon	television
헤어드라이어	he-eodeurai-eo	hair dryer

9. 고기류 Meat

달걀	dalgyal	egg
닭고기	dakgogi	chicken
돼지고기	dwaejigogi	pork
불고기	bulgogi	bulgogi
소시지	sosiji	sausage
소고기	sogogi	beef
양고기	yanggogi	lamb
햄	haem	ham

10. 해산물 Seafood

갈치	galchi	hairtail
게	ge	crab
고등어	godeung-eo	mackerel
굴	gul	oyster
김	gim	seaweed
멸치	myeolchi	anchovy
미역	miyeok	seaweed
새우	saeu	shrimp
연어	yeoneo	salmon
오징어	ojing eo	squid
장어	jang-eo	eel
조개	jogae	clam

11. 채소 Vegetables

가지	gaji	eggplant
감자	gamja	potato
고구마	goguma	sweet potato
고추	gochu	chili pepper
깻잎	kkaennip	perilla leaves
당근	danggeun	carrot
마늘	maneul	garlic
무	mu	radish
배추	baechu	napa cabbage
버섯	beoseot	mushroom
부추	buchu	chives
브로콜리	beurokolli	broccoli
상추	sangchu	lettuce
생강	saenggang	ginger
시금치	sigeumchi	spinach
양배추	yangbaechu	cabbage
양파	yangpa	onion
오이	oi	cucumber
콩	kong	bean
콩나물	kongnamul	bean sprouts
토마토	tomato	tomato
파	pa	green onion
피망	pimang	bell pepper
호박	hobak	pumpkin

12. 과일 Fruits

귤	gyul	tangerine
딸기	ttalgi	strawberry
레몬	remon	lemon
멜론	mellon	melon
바나나	banana	banana
밤	bam	chestnut
배	bae	pear
복숭아	boksunga	peach
사과	sagwa	apple
수박	subak	watermelon
오렌지	orenji	orange
체리	cheri	cherry
키위	kiwi	kiwi
파인애플	painaepeul	pineapple
포도	podo	grape

13. 간식 Snacks

과자	gwaja	snack
떡	tteok	rice cake
사탕	satang	candy
아이스크림	alseukeurim	ice cream
젤리	jelli	jelly
초콜릿	chokollit	chocolate
케이크	keikeu	cake
쿠키	kuki	cookie

녹차	nokcha	green tea
레모네이드	remoneideu	lemonade
물	mul	water
사이다	saida	cider
스무디	seumudi	smoothie
아이스티	aiseuti	iced tea
주스	juseu	juice
커피	keopi	coffee
콜라	kolla	cola
탄산수	tansansu	sparkling water
핫초코	hatchoko	hot chocolate
홍차	hongcha	black tea

15. 술 Alcoholic beverages

막걸리	makgeolli	makgeolli
맥주	maekju	beer
보드카	bodeuka	vodka
샴페인	syampein	champagne
생맥주	saengmaekju	draft beer
소주	soju	soju
와인	wain	wine
위스키	wiseuki	whiskey
청주	cheongju	cheongju
칵테일	kakteil	cocktail
하이볼	haibol	highball

계산	gyesan	bill
계산서	gyesanseo	receipt
대기	daegi	waiting
대표 메뉴	daepyo menyu	signature dish
레스토랑	reseutorang	restaurant
메뉴	menyu	menu
분위기	bunwigi	atmosphere
세트 메뉴	seteu menyu	set menu
수저	sujeo	spoon and chopsticks
숟가락	sutgarak	spoon
앞치마	apchima	apron
예약	yeyak	reservation
외식	oesik	eating out
요리사	yorisa	chef
점원	jeomwon	waiter
접시	jeopsi	plate
젓가락	jeotgarak	chopsticks
종업원	jong-eobwon	server
주문	jumun	order
카운터	kauntco	counter
컵	keop	cup
코스 요리	koscu yori	course meal
포크	pokeu	fork
후식	husik	dessert

Vocabulary

경찰서	gyeongchalseo	police station
계단	gyedan	stairs
교회	gyohoe	church
꽃집	kkotjip	flower shop
다리	dari	bridge
미술관	misulgwan	art gallery
대사관	daesagwan	embassy
박물관	bangmulgwan	museum
병원	byeongwon	hospital
빌딩	bilding	building
소방서	sobangseo	fire station
시청	sicheong	city hall
실내	sillae	indoor
실외	siroe	outdoor
아파트	apateu	apartment
예식장	yesikjang	wedding hall
우체국	ucheguk	post office
육교	yukgyo	pedestrian overpass
절	jeol	temple
지하	jiha	underground
헬스클럽	helseukeulleop	gym
호텔	hotel	hotel
회사	hoesa	company
휴게실	hyugesil	lounge

가이드	gaideu	guide
가이드북	gaideubuk	guidebook
경치	gyeongchi	scenery
관광	gwangwang	sightseeing
관광 안내소	gwangwang annaeso	tourist information center
국내 여행	gungnae yeohaeng	domestic travel
기념관	ginyeomgwan	memorial hall
기념품	ginyeompum	souvenir
면세점	myeonsejeom	duty-free shop
박물관	bangmulgwan	museum
배낭	baenang	backpack
배낭여행	baenangyeohaeng	backpacking
비자	bija	visa
시차	sicha	time difference
신혼여행	sinhonnyeohaeng	honeymoon
여권	yeogwon	passport
여행사	yeohaengsa	travel agency
여행자 보험	yeohaengja boheom	travel insurance
왕복	wangbok	round trip
일정	iljeong	itinerary
입국	ipguk	entry
출국	chulguk	departure
패키지여행	paekijiyeohaeng	package tour
해외여행	hae-oeyeohaeng	overseas travel

19. 교통 수단 Transportation

개찰구	gaechalgu	ticket gate
고속도로	gosokdoro	highway
교통 신호	gyotong sinho	traffic signal
노약자석	noyakjaseok	priority seat
기차	gicha	train
막차	makcha	last train
매점	maejeom	convenience store
매표소	maepyoso	ticket office
목적지	mokjeokji	destination
배	bae	ship
버스	beoseu	bus
비행기	bihaenggi	airplane
신호등	sinhodeung	traffic light
왕복	wangbok	round trip
요금	yogeum	fare
자가용	jagayong	private car
자동차	jadongcha	car
자전거	jajeongeo	bicycle
지하철	jihacheol	subway
직행	jikaeng	express
택시	taeksi	taxi
편도	pyeondo	one way
항공	hanggong	aviation
~호선	~hoseon	line (subway)

20. 미용 Beauty

각질 제거	gakjil jegeo	exfoliation
네일 케어	neil ke-eo	nail care
마사지	masaji	massage
마스크팩	maseukeupaek	face mask
머리하다	meorihada	to do hair
미용	miyong	beauty
미용실	miyongsil	beauty salon
바디로션	badirosyeon	body lotion
바르다	bareuda	to apply
보습	boseup	moisturize
샴푸	syampu	shampoo
성형	seonghyeong	plastic surgery
스파	seupa	spa
염색	yeomsaek	dye
유행	yuhaeng	trend
이발	ibal	haircut
자르다	jareuda	to cut
제모	jemo	hair removal
클렌징	keullenjing	cleansing
파마	pama	perm
피부과	pibugwa	dermatology
피부 관리	pibu gwalli	skin care
향수	hyangsu	perfume
화장	hwajang	makeup

골프	golpeu	golf
결승	gyeolseung	final
농구	nonggu	basketball
무승부	museungbu	tie
배구	baegu	volleyball
배드민턴	baedeuminteon	badminton
수영	suyeong	swimming
스케이트	seukeiteu	skating
스키	seuki	skiing
아마추어	amachueo	amateur
아시안게임	asiangeim	Asian Games
야구	yagu	baseball
올림픽	ollimpik	Olympics
월드컵	woldeukeop	World Cup
유도	yudo	judo
응원	eungwon	cheering
준결승	jungyeolseung	semifinal
축구	chukgu	soccer
탁구	takgu	table tennis
태권도	taegwondo	taekwondo
테니스	teniseu	tennis
풋볼	putbol	football
프로 선수	peuro seonsu	professional player
하키	haki	hockey

감독	gamdok	director
공연	gongyeon	performance
관객	gwangaek	audience
극장	geukjang	theater
극본	geukbon	script
리허설	riheoseol	rehearsal
매진	maejin	sold out
무대	mudae	stage
배우	bae-u	actor
상영	sang-yeong	screening
소극장	sogeukjang	small theater
시나리오	sinario	script
연극	yeongeuk	play
연출	yeonchul	directing
예매	yemae	reservation
자막	jamak	subtitles
장면	jangmyeon	scene
제작	jejak	production
조명	jomyeong	lighting
주연	juyeon	lead role
조연	joyeon	supporting role
촬영	chwaryeong	filming
편집	pyeonjip	editing
흥행	heunghaeng	box office success

23. 대중매체 Mass media

광고	gwanggo	advertisement
뉴스	nyuseu	news
드라마	deurama	drama
라디오	radio	radio
미디어	midieo	media
방송	bangsong	broadcast
시청자	sicheongja	viewer
신문	sinmun	newspaper
언론	eollon	press
인터넷	inteonet	internet
잡지	japji	magazine
홍보	hongbo	publicity

24. 학교 School

유치원	yuchiwon	kindergarten
초등학교	chodeunghakgyo	elementary school
중학교	junghakgyo	middle school
고등학교	godeunghakgyo	high school
대학교	daehakgyo	university
대학원	daehagwon	graduate school
교문	gyomun	school gate
교실	gyosil	classroom
결석	gyeolseok	absence
기숙사	gisuksa	dormitory
방학	banghak	vacation

선생님	seonsaengnim	teacher
시험	siheom	exam
유학	yuhak	study abroad
장학금	janghakgeum	scholarship
전공	jeongong	major
졸업식	joreopsik	graduation ceremony
지각	jigak	tardiness
출석	chulseok	attendance
학기	hakgi	semester
학년	hangnyeon	grade (school year)
학비	hakbi	tuition
학생	haksaeng	student

25. 학습 도구 Learning tools

공책	gongchaek	notebook
교과서	gyogwaseo	textbook
노트	noteu	notepad
볼펜	bolpen	ballpoint pen
사전	sajeon	dictionary
수첩	sucheop	memo pad
연필	yeonpil	pencil
종이	jong-i	paper
지우개	jiugae	eraser
책	chaek	book
필통	piltong	pencil case
형광펜	hyeonggwangpen	highlighter

갈아입다	garaipda	to change clothes
꿈을 꾸다	kkumeul kkuda	to dream
눕다	nupda	to lie down
만나다	mannada	to meet
목욕하다	mogyokada	to take a bath
빨래하다	ppallaehada	to do laundry
산책하다	sanchaekada	to take a walk
샤워하다	syawohada	to shower
생활하다	saenghwalhada	to live
세수하다	sesuhada	to wash one's face
쇼핑하다	syopinghada	to go shopping
쉬다	swida	to rest
스트레칭	seuteureching	stretch
식사하다	siksahada	to have a meal
아침	achim	morning
양치질	yangchijil	brushing one's teeth
외출하다	oechulhada	to go out
운동하다	undonghada	to exercise
잠	jam	sleep
저녁	jeonyeok	evening
점심	jeomsim	lunch
청소하다	cheongsohada	to clean
취미	chwimi	hobby
피곤	pigon	tired

근무하다	geunmuhada	to work
동료	dongnyo	colleague
면접	myeonjeop	interview
방문하다	bangmunhada	to visit
복사	boksa	copy
사무실	samusil	office
사장	sajang	president (of a company)
서류	seoryu	document
수고	sugo	effort
스트레스	seuteureseu	stress
승진하다	seungjinhada	to get promoted
실례	sillye	excuse me
실수	silsu	mistake
아르바이트	areubaiteu	part-time job
일	il	work
직원	jigwon	employee
직장	jikjang	workplace
출근	chulgeun	going to work
출장	chuljang	business trip
퇴근	toegeun	leaving work
회식	hoesik	company dinner
회의	hoeui	meeting
휴가	hyuga	vacation

28. 직종 Occupations

간호사	ganhosa	nurse
감독	gamdok	director
경찰관	gyeongchalgwan	police officer
교사	gyosa	teacher
교수	gyosu	professor
대통령	daetongnyeong	president
목수	moksu	carpenter
배우	bae-u	actor
번역가	beonyeokga	translator
변호사	byeonhosa	lawyer
비행기 조종사	bihaenggi jojongsa	pilot
어부	eobu	fisherman
엔지니어	enjinieo	engineer
요리사	yorisa	chef
운동선수	undongseonsu	athlete
운전기사	unjeongisa	driver
음악가	eumakga	musician
의사	uisa	doctor
자영업자	jayeong-eopja	self-employed
작가	jakga	writer
통역사	tong-yeoksa	interpreter
프로그래머	peurogeuraemeo	programmer
화가	hwaga	painter
회계사	hoegyesa	accountant

가슴	gaseum	chest
귀	gwi	ear
눈	nun	eye
눈썹	nunsseop	eyebrow
다리	dari	leg
등	deung	back
머리	meori	head
목	mok	neck
무릎	mureup	knee
발	bal	foot
발목	balmok	ankle
배	bae	stomach
뼈	ppyeo	bone
손	son	hand
손가락	songarak	finger
심장	simjang	heart
어깨	eokkae	shoulder
얼굴	eolgul	face
엉덩이	eongdeong-i	hip
위	wi	stomach
이	i	tooth
입	ip	mouth
입술	ipsul	lip
장	jang	intestine

Vocabulary

코	ko	nose
피부	pibu	skin
허리	heori	waist, lower back

30. 병원/약국 Hospital/Pharmacy

건강	geongang	health
내과	naegwa	internal medicine
넘어지다	neomeojida	to fall down
다치다	dachida	to get hurt
밴드	baendeu	band-aid
병	byeong	disease
붕대	bungdae	bandage
상처	sangcheo	wound
소독약	sodongnyak	antiseptic
소아과	soagwa	pediatrics
소화제	sohwaje	digestive medicine
안과	angwa	ophthalmology
안약	anyak	eye drops
약사	yaksa	pharmacist
엑스레이	ekseurei	X-ray
이비인후과	ibiinhugwa	otolaryngology
입원	ibwon	hospitalization
정형외과	jeonghyeongoegwa	orthopedics
주사	jusa	injection
진찰	jinchal	examination
처방	cheobang	prescription

치과	chigwa	dentistry
치료	chiryo	treatment
환자	hwanja	patient

31. 증상/증세 Symptoms/Conditions

기침	gichim	cough
나다	nada	to occur
낫다	natda	to get better
땀	ttam	sweat
배탈	baetal	upset stomach
붓다	butda	to swell
설사	seolsa	diarrhea
소화	sohwa	digestion
숨	sum	breath
심하다	simhada	to be severe
아프다	apeuda	to hurt
약하다	yakada	to be weak
열	yeol	fever
콧물	konmul	runny nose
편찮다	pyeonchanta	to be ill (formal)

- **긴급 구조** Emergency Services: 119
화재, 응급 의료 상황, 구조가 필요한 경우. (For fires, medical emergencies, and rescue situations.)

- **경찰** Police: 112
범죄 신고, 치안 문제, 긴급 상황이 발생했을 때. (To report crimes, security issues, and urgent situations.)

- **외국인 종합안내센터** Korea Travel Hotline: 1330
24시간 운영, 관광 정보, 통역 서비스 제공. (Operates 24/7, travel information and interpretation services.)

- **외교부 영사콜센터** Ministry of Foreign Affairs Consular Call Center: 02-3210-0404
외국인이 긴급 상황에 처했을 때, 여권을 잃어버렸을 때, 그 외 상담이 필요할 때. (For emergencies involving foreigners, lost passports, and other consular support.)

- **외국인 주민센터** Foreigner Support Center: 1345
외국인 생활 지원, 법률 상담, 통역 서비스. (Provides support for foreign residents, legal counseling, and interpretation services.)

- **다산콜센터** Dasan Call Foundation: (02)120
서울 생활과 여행에 관한 일반 정보 제공. 교통수단, 시청 등 관공서 운영 시간, 공공시설 이용, 문화 행사 안내 등. (Provides general information on living and tourism in Seoul, including public transportation, business operation of City Hall and district offices, public facility use, cultural events, etc.)

감수

Jamie Lypka

고려대학교 국제대학원 국제학 석사 (국제평화안보)
MA, International Studies (Peace & Security), Korea University
아메리칸 대학교 국제 관계학과 석사 (국제비교학 – 동아시아)
American University, School of International Service, MA in Comparative and Regional Studies (East Asia)
현) 한국국제교류재단 – 선임 편집자 (2019~)
The Korea Foundation – Senior Copyeditor
전) 서울대학교 언어교육원 TEPS 센터 – 교열원, 연구원 (2014~2018)
TEPS Center, Seoul National University – Researcher/Editor

Useful Korean Travel Phrases

초판 / 2024년 10월 25일

발행인 / 이기선

발행처 / 제이플러스

주소 / 경기도 고양시 덕양구 향동로 217 KA1312

영업부 / 02-332-8320 편집부 / 02-3142-2520

홈페이지 / www.jplus114.com

등록번호 / 제 10-1680호

등록일자 / 1998년 12월 9일

ISBN / 979-11-5601-268-9

＊피본은 구입하신 서점이나 본사에서 바꾸어 드립니다.
＊책에 대한 의견, 출판 희망 도서가 있으시면 홈페이지에 글을 남겨 주세요.